DISCIPLING THROUGH
PHILIPPIANS

ANDREW WOMMACK

Unless otherwise indicated, all Scripture quotations are taken from the *King James Version* of the Bible in the public domain.

The author has emphasized some words in Scripture quotations with underline.

Discipling Through Philippians
ISBN 13: 978-1-59548-546-5
eBook ISBN 13: 978-1-68031-920-0

Copyright © 2012 by Andrew Wommack Ministries Inc.
PO Box 3333
Colorado Springs CO 80934-3333

awmi.net

All rights reserved under International Copyright Law. Contents and/or cover may not be reproduced in whole or in part in any form without the express written consent of the Publisher.

ABOUT THIS BOOK

The notes in this book have been taken from both the *Life for Today Study Bible – Galatians, Ephesians, Philippians & Colossians Edition* and the *Living Commentary* software program. Years of study, meditation, and revelation have gone into these writings. They are designed to instruct and inspire you. As you consider the information and wisdom presented here, you will receive a deeper understanding of the book of Philippians—a book rife with rejoicing and thankfulness, a book with the potential to thoroughly alter your perception of life.

The *Life for Today* series is the product of years of research and study. It has been a part of Andrew's ministry for some time and was first offered over a decade ago. In an effort to make this knowledge available to as many people as possible, *Life for Today* has been incorporated into the *Living Commentary* program. The *Living Commentary* program shares some similarities with *Life for Today*—it, too, is a Bible commentary, an almost verse-by-verse study of God's Word. However, the *Living Commentary* covers passages from the entire Bible and is comprised of Andrew's study from recent years, whereas *Life for Today* focuses on the first half of the New Testament and was completed some years ago.

Since *Life for Today* is the precursor to the *Living Commentary*, some points made in the *Living Commentary* build on information provided by *Life for Today*. All of this information has been given to you in this book for your benefit and instruction. Carefully consider everything presented to you. The teaching given here has the power to completely change your life!

INTRODUCTION TO PHILIPPIANS

(Taken from the *Life for Today Study Bible – Galatians, Ephesians, Philippians, and Colossians Edition*)

The letter to the Philippians is one of four written by Paul while he was in prison. The other three are Ephesians, Colossians, and Philemon. Philippians was written to the first church established by Paul in Europe, in what was then known as the province of Macedonia. Paul visited Philippi on his second missionary journey after receiving a night vision where he saw a man from Macedonia standing before him, earnestly asking him to **"come over into Macedonia, and help us"** (Acts 16:9).

After receiving this vision, Paul and his companion, Silas (Acts 15:40), immediately endeavored to go into Macedonia, concluding that God had called them to preach the Gospel to the people there (Acts 16:10). Paul crossed over into Europe, stopping first at Philippi (Acts 16:12). The Scripture records the meeting and conversion of several people at Philippi. Among them was Lydia, a woman of the city of Thyatira (Acts 16:14) whose heart was open to the Lord. She was baptized along with her whole household and was faithful to the Lord (Acts 16:13-15).

Paul cast a demon out of a girl who was possessed with a spirit of divination, and this led to both him and Silas being cast into prison (Acts 16:16-23). This is the incident where Paul and Silas praised God at midnight while their feet were fastened in stocks. The Lord sent an earthquake, opened all the prison cells, and loosed all the prisoners' bands, but not a single prisoner tried to escape. This led to the conversion of the jailer along with his whole family (Acts 16:30-34). There were many other members of the Philippian church who knew Paul but whose stories and conversions we do not know.

Paul's primary reason for writing this letter was to thank the Philippian church for the gift they had sent him in his time of need (Phil. 4:10-19). He also used this opportunity to encourage them to look confidently to Christ for their joy and unity, and to continue to persevere in their Christian life and faith.

Even though Paul wrote this letter from prison, it contains a constant theme of rejoicing. The words **"joy"** and **"rejoice"** were used sixteen times in this short epistle. Paul made it very clear in Philippians 3 that his personal relationship with the Lord was the key factor in his joy.

Paul had a special affection for the Philippians. They were not only the first fruits of his ministry in Europe but also the only church that contributed to his ministry after he had departed from their city (Phil. 4:15-16).

It is supposed that Paul wrote what we call the second letter to the Corinthians while he was in Philippi.

Recipients of Paul's Epistle "Philippians"

The Roman colony of Philippi was located in northern Greece (called Macedonia in Paul's day). It was a thriving commercial center at the crossroads between Europe and Asia. The Philippian church displayed a strong missionary zeal. It consisted mostly of Gentile believers; therefore, Paul did not specifically quote any Old Testament passages in this letter.

Date and Place of Writing

Philippians was probably written to the church at Philippi from Rome sometime in early A.D. 63. This can be deduced from the fact that Paul was imprisoned in Rome during A.D. 62-63. In this letter to the Philippians, Paul mentioned that they had sent offerings to him by Epaphroditus (Phil. 4:18). While in Rome, Epaphroditus fell sick, and enough time elapsed for word of that to filter back to Philippi (Phil. 2:26-27). More time elapsed as Paul learned of their concern for Epaphroditus' health. Therefore, it is reasonable to assume that this letter to the Philippians, which Paul sent by the hand of Epaphroditus, happened at least one year after Paul arrived in Rome.

About the Author

Paul is clearly the author of this epistle, as stated in Philippians 1:1.

PHILIPPIANS 1

Paul and Timotheus, the servants of Jesus Christ, to all the saints in Christ Jesus which are at Philippi, with the bishops and deacons:

PHILIPPIANS 1:1

LIFE FOR TODAY STUDY BIBLE NOTES:

• Although Timothy's name was used with the Apostle Paul's as a fellow sender of this letter, Timothy was probably not a co-author. Throughout this letter, when Timothy is mentioned, he is spoken of in the third person (Phil. 2:19-24). Paul was the author, and he simply included Timothy in the greeting because Timothy had ministered with him in Philippi and knew these people.

• Paul opened this letter not with a list of all his accomplishments and virtues but by identifying himself as a slave of Jesus Christ (Greek: *doulos* – "a slave (literal or figurative, involuntary or voluntary; frequently, therefore in a sense of subjection or subservience)" [*Strong's Concordance*]). Carnal people use their past accomplishments to impress others and open doors. Godly people are not out to impress others with themselves, but with who their Master is. Paul was prouder of his Master than he was of his service to his Master.

Paul was quick to note that Jesus had elevated the Philippians to the position of **"saints."** As believers, we all have been made saints through what Jesus did for us, but not all of us have become slaves. Slavery to Christ is our **"reasonable service"** (Rom. 12:1), but it is voluntary. Faith in Christ as Savior is essential for salvation, and submission to Christ as Lord is essential for victory and true joy in this life.

LIVING COMMENTARY NOTE:

Timothy was present with Paul while he was incarcerated in Rome, as can be seen by the passage in Philippians 2:19, which reads, **"But I trust in the Lord Jesus to send Timotheus shortly unto you, that I also may be of good comfort, when I know your state."**

Philip of Macedon, the father of Alexander the Great, conquered the city of Crenides and named it after himself, Philippi. Paul first preached the Gospel in Europe in Philippi, where Lydia and others responded to his message (Acts 16:14). Philippi was where Paul and Silas were beaten and thrown in jail, and sang praises to God at midnight in the dungeon (Acts 16:22-25). The Lord sent an earthquake that broke all the prisoners' chains and opened their cell doors, but none of them escaped (Acts 16:26-28). The jailer received salvation as a result (Acts 16:30-33).

PHILIPPIANS 1:1 *(Continued)*

LIFE FOR TODAY STUDY BIBLE NOTES:

• Paul mentioned two special groups of people in this verse: bishops and deacons. The word **"bishop"** is derived from the Greek word *episkopos*. This Greek word was translated **"overseers"** in Acts 20:28. The word **"deacon"** (Greek: *diakonos*) was probably derived from the Greek word *diako*. *Diako* means "to run on errands" (*Strong's Concordance*). The *King James Version* translated **"deacon"** elsewhere as **"servant"** or **"servants"** (Matt. 22:13, 23:11; Mark 9:35; John 2:5, 9, 12:26; Rom. 16:1, and 27 [subscript]), and **"minister"** or **"ministers"** (Matt. 20:26; Mark 10:43; Rom. 13:4, 15:8; 1 Cor. 3:5; 2 Cor. 3:6, 6:4, 11:15, 23; Gal. 2:17; Eph. 3:7, 6:21; Col. 1:7, 23, 25, 4:7; 1 Thess. 3:2; and 1 Tim. 4:6).

The early New Testament church was organized. The **"bishop"** and the **"deacon"** were leadership positions.

• The bishops and deacons were the leadership of the church at Philippi. Notice that those outside of leadership were called saints. This clearly identifies every believer as a saint. There is no scriptural basis for elevating just a few Christians to an elite status of sainthood.

DISCIPLESHIP QUESTIONS

1. What happened to Paul and Silas in Philippi?

2. How did Paul introduce himself in this letter?

3. *Discussion question:* What does being a slave of Jesus Christ mean to you?

4. *Discussion question:* How do you view the concept of a "saint," and how does this line up with the Word?

Grace be unto you, and peace, from God our Father, and from the Lord Jesus Christ.

PHILIPPIANS 1:2

LIFE FOR TODAY STUDY BIBLE NOTES:

- The only way we can experience true peace is through being reconciled to God by grace. Grace and peace always go together.

LIVING COMMENTARY NOTE:

There can be no true peace without the grace of God. Romans 5:1 says, **"Therefore being justified by faith, we have peace with God through our Lord Jesus Christ."** True grace and peace only come through the proper knowledge of what God has done for us. Second Peter 1:2 says, **"Grace and peace be multiplied unto you through the knowledge of God, and of Jesus our Lord."**

DISCIPLESHIP QUESTIONS

1. From whom do grace and peace come?

2. Romans 5:1 says, **"Therefore being _____ _____ _____, we have peace with God through our Lord Jesus Christ."**

3. What is the only way you can experience true peace?

4. *Discussion question:* In what ways can you apply 2 Peter 1:2 to your life?

I thank my God upon every remembrance of you,

PHILIPPIANS 1:3

LIFE FOR TODAY STUDY BIBLE NOTES:

• The proper motivation for all ministry is love for God. If ministers only shared the Word because of the friendships they could make and other positive benefits, they wouldn't be ministering long. Be that as it may, it is wonderful when the Gospel is received and relationships are made. Paul expressed some of that joy here.

The Philippians were some of Paul's closest friends, and it shows in this statement. He rejoiced every time he thought of them. That's quite a testimony. I'm sure there were other groups he ministered to that didn't bring a smile to his face when he thought of them. The Philippians had supported Paul more than any other church (Phil. 4:15-16).

• The Greek word *mneia*, which was translated **"remembrance"** here, was also translated **"mention"** in Romans 1:9, Ephesians 1:16, and Philemon 4. In each of those instances, it is clear that Paul was speaking of praying for those people. In this instance, Paul went on to mention his prayers for the Philippians (Phil. 1:4), so the remembrances he was referring to here were times of prayer. As he prayed and the Philippians came to his mind, he always rejoiced for the fellowship he had with them in the Gospel (Phil. 1:5).

LIVING COMMENTARY NOTE:

I bet there were groups of people Paul had ministered to that he didn't thank God for every time he thought of them. This means these Philippians were special to Paul. He mentioned in Philippians 4:15-16 that these were the only people who supported his ministry after he left them. Certainly, this was one thing that endeared these people to him. These Philippians were his partners (see my note at Phil. 1:5).

DISCIPLESHIP QUESTIONS

1. How can the relationship between Paul and the Philippians be described?

2. *Discussion question:* The proper motivation for ministry is love for God. What sort of effect can this have when done properly and when not done properly?

Always in every prayer of mine for you all making request with joy,

PHILIPPIANS 1:4

LIFE FOR TODAY STUDY BIBLE NOTES:

• Certainly, Paul was a man who was in communion with God. Therefore, for Paul to remember the Philippians **"always in every prayer"** was very often. This attests to the love that Paul had for the Philippians (see my note at Phil. 1:3).

LIVING COMMENTARY NOTE:

Paul prayed for these Philippians every time he prayed.

DISCIPLESHIP QUESTIONS

1. What was one way Paul showed his love for the Philippians?

2. *Discussion question:* Why should there be someone you remember **"always in every prayer"**?

For your fellowship in the gospel from the first day until now;

PHILIPPIANS 1:5

LIFE FOR TODAY STUDY BIBLE NOTES:

- Why is it that Paul had such joy and thanksgiving every time he thought of the Philippians? He gave the answer here. It was because of their **"fellowship in the gospel."** The word **"fellowship"** was translated from the Greek word *koinonia*, and this Greek word means "partnership, i.e. (literally) participation" (*Strong's Concordance*). This word was translated **"contribution"** in Romans 15:26 and **"distribution"** in 2 Corinthians 9:13. Both of these words were dealing with finances.

Paul very clearly stated later in this same letter (Phil. 4:15-16) that the Philippians were the only church that supported him in the beginning of his ministry. One of the reasons Paul had such fond thoughts about the Philippians was that they had sacrificially supported him with their finances. Certainly, other things were involved, but finances were one of the important ways the Philippians showed their love and support for Paul.

- As explained in the previous *Life for Today* note at this verse, Paul was referring to the Philippians' support for him, including financial contributions. Here, he said that this support was **"from the first day until now."** Certainly, one of the things that caused Paul to rejoice every time he thought of the Philippians was their faithfulness over a period of time.

LIVING COMMENTARY NOTE:

The Greek word that was translated **"fellowship"** in this verse was *koinonia*, and it literally means "partnership" (*Strong's Concordance*). It was translated **"partnership"** in this verse in the *New International Version*. Paul was speaking of the fact that these people had supported him financially after he left their area. He made reference to this in Philippians 4. Certainly, this was one of the reasons Paul thanked God every time he thought of the Philippians.

PHILIPPIANS 1:5 *(Continued)*

LIFE FOR TODAY
STUDY BIBLE NOTES:

It is a blessing to have people express their love to any degree, but sad to say, this type of fellowship doesn't typically last very long. Partnerships are hard to maintain. Many things work against partnerships, and most don't last long. It is a real joy to ministers to have people who were ministered to many years ago remember them and still support the work they are doing.

DISCIPLESHIP QUESTIONS

1. How did the Philippians show their partnership with Paul?

2. *Discussion question:* Why do you think finances make a difference in building a partnership?

Being confident of this very thing, that he which hath begun a good work in you will perform it until the day of Jesus Christ:

PHILIPPIANS 1:6

LIFE FOR TODAY STUDY BIBLE NOTES:

- Paul had confidence in the Lord that what He had started in the Philippians, He would also continue and complete. That is not to say that the Philippians' success was automatic; believers have to cooperate with what God wants to do in their lives. Man's faithfulness may always be suspect, but God's faithfulness is never in question. It is always God's will to continue and complete the good work that He begins in His children.

- **"The day of Jesus Christ"** that Paul was speaking of here is the second coming of Christ. Paul was confident that the salvation given to them through faith in Christ would be secure until Christ returned and their physical bodies were changed into His image (Phil. 3:21).

LIVING COMMENTARY NOTE:

It isn't true that every person who has ever had God start a good work in them sees it come to perfection. This isn't really for every person. This was a statement made to people who were partners with Paul—people who were not just takers but had moved into the realm of givers. They weren't just thinking of themselves; they were demonstrating the love of Jesus by showing love toward others through their giving. Paul was absolutely confident that for people like that—who are demonstrating a cooperation with the Holy Spirit's leading for their lives—God would bring to completion the good things He had begun in them.

DISCIPLESHIP QUESTIONS

1. Who is this verse for?

2. Is God's faithfulness ever in question?

3. What does **"the day of Jesus Christ"** refer to?

Even as it is meet for me to think this of you all, because I have you in my heart; inasmuch as both in my bonds, and in the defence and confirmation of the gospel, ye all are partakers of my grace.

PHILIPPIANS 1:7

LIFE FOR TODAY STUDY BIBLE NOTES:

• It was right for the Apostle Paul to be confident that the good work begun in the Philippian believers would continue, because they had become partakers of the same grace that Paul had. Paul knew firsthand just how strong the grace of God was, and he knew it would sustain the Philippians. It had worked for him, and it would work for them as well.

LIVING COMMENTARY NOTE:

Paul expressing the confidence toward these Philippians he spoke of in Philippians 1:6 was right because they were in his heart. This meant he prayed for them and loved them. They had received the same grace he had received, and he knew God was completing the work begun in him. So, that same grace and Holy Spirit would accomplish the same in them.

DISCIPLESHIP QUESTIONS

1. *Discussion question:* What are some examples of how God's grace has shown you He is completing the work He's begun in you?

For God is my record, how greatly I long after you all in the bowels of Jesus Christ.

PHILIPPIANS 1:8

LIFE FOR TODAY STUDY BIBLE NOTES:

• **"For God is my record"** is an expression that Paul used to convey the fact that God was the one who really knew and could testify to the truthfulness of what was in Paul's heart. This strengthens the truthfulness of Paul's statement. Similar expressions used by Paul are found in Romans 1:9; 2 Corinthians 1:23; 1 Thessalonians 2:5, and 10.

• The Greek word *splagchnon*, translated **"bowels"** here, was also translated **"tender mercy"** in Luke 1:78. The *New International Version* rendered this word as **"affection"** in this verse. The belief of Paul's day was that the seat of the affections was located in the bowels of a person. Today we speak of the heart as being the seat of our emotions. Neither one of these words are to be taken literally. It is speaking of our emotions.

LIVING COMMENTARY NOTE:

Paul loved the people he ministered to. The sacrifices he made in ministry were not for himself. It wasn't so he could have a bigger ministry but that so more people could experience God's love. The motives behind our actions are more important than our actions themselves.

DISCIPLESHIP QUESTIONS

1. *Discussion question:* Paul loved the people he ministered to. What difference could it make in the body of Christ if more people had this attitude?

2. The _____ behind your actions are more _____ than the actions themselves.

3. What is **"bowels"** referring to in this verse?

And this I pray, that your love may abound yet more and more in knowledge and in all judgment;

PHILIPPIANS 1:9

LIFE FOR TODAY STUDY BIBLE NOTES:

• As Peter so aptly put it in 2 Peter 1:3, **"his divine power hath given unto us all things that pertain unto life and godliness, through the knowledge of him."** Even love is based on knowledge. Our love can be increased with the correct knowledge and diminished with the wrong knowledge.

We have all experienced an increased love for someone as we learn of some special thing that person has done for us. Likewise, we have all experienced a loss of love when we have discovered things that someone we love has done to hurt us. Our knowledge influences our emotions. The more we know of God and His ways, the more our love for God and others will abound.

• The knowledge that is being spoken of here is spiritual understanding of God's love. Judgment is the ability to use or apply that knowledge correctly. Paul was saying that as we gain spiritual understanding of God's love and learn to apply it correctly in our relationships, then the manifestation of God's love in our lives will increase dramatically.

LIVING COMMENTARY NOTE:

The way our love increases is through **"knowledge and…judgment."** The word **"knowledge"** in this verse was translated from the Greek word *epignosis*. That word means "recognition, i.e. (by implication) full discernment, acknowledgement" (*Strong's Concordance*). This is the same Greek word that was translated **"acknowledging"** in Philemon 6, which says, **"That the communication of thy faith may become effectual by the acknowledging of every good thing which is in you in Christ Jesus."** The Greek word *aisthesis*, which was translated **"judgment"** here in Philippians 1:9, means "perception, i.e. (figuratively) discernment" (*Strong's Concordance*).

Our love for God and others doesn't increase by experiences or touches from God. It increases proportionally to how much we know and discern God's love for us. Experiences can be a part of that process, but wrong knowledge will lead to wrong understanding, which will affect our love walk.

PHILIPPIANS 1:9 *(Continued)*

DISCIPLESHIP QUESTIONS

1. If your love for God and others doesn't increase by experiences or touches from God, what does it increase in proportion to?

2. Second Peter 1:3 says, **"His divine power _____ given unto us _____ _____ that pertain unto life and godliness, through the _____ of him."**

3. What will happen the more you know of God and His ways?

4. *Discussion question:* The knowledge spoken of in this verse is spiritual understanding of God's love, and judgment is the ability to use or apply that knowledge correctly. In what areas of your life have you exercised judgment, as used here?

That ye may approve things that are excellent; that ye may be sincere and without offence till the day of Christ;

PHILIPPIANS 1:10

LIFE FOR TODAY STUDY BIBLE NOTES:

• The *New International Version* translated this phrase, **"ye may approve things that are excellent,"** as **"you may be able to discern what is best."** Paul was saying that increasing our understanding and application (see my note at Phil. 1:9) of God's love will cause us to have better discernment about right and wrong.

• All of the things listed in Philippians 1:10-11 are the results of having our love abound through knowledge and judgment (Phil. 1:9). We receive the love of God through faith at salvation. We then increase our experience of God's love through knowledge and judgment. This leads to better discernment of what's right and wrong (see the previous *Life for Today* note at this verse), and produces sincerity (pureness) that results in us walking without offense. If these things are working in us, then the fruits of righteousness follow, causing glory and praise to God (Phil. 1:11).

LIVING COMMENTARY NOTE:

Paul was praying that the Philippians' acknowledgement of God's love would abound. That would lead to them become genuine and sincere and without offense until the day the Lord comes. That will work the same way for us today. Those who are falling into sin aren't perfecting God's love in them.

DISCIPLESHIP QUESTIONS

1. Those who are falling into sin aren't doing what?

2. *Discussion question:* What areas, if any, do you think could use improvement regarding offences, and how would you go about making those improvements?

Being filled with the fruits of righteousness, which are by Jesus Christ, unto the glory and praise of God.

PHILIPPIANS 1:11

LIVING COMMENTARY NOTE:

All the fruits of righteousness come from God's love. If we want more fruit, we need to focus more on the love of God. See my notes at Philippians 1:9-10.

DISCIPLESHIP QUESTIONS

1. If you focus more on the love of God, what will that produce?

But I would ye should understand, brethren, that the things which happened unto me have fallen out rather unto the furtherance of the gospel;

PHILIPPIANS 1:12

LIFE FOR TODAY STUDY BIBLE NOTES:

- Paul, the prisoner, was trying to comfort those who were not in prison. He didn't want them to feel badly about his situation, so he tried to get them to look at things the way he did. His imprisonment was worth it because it advanced the kingdom of God. Most people would find this of little comfort, because most people are more concerned with advancing themselves than they are with advancing the kingdom of God. Paul's heart and focus were so fixed on God that any price he had to pay, even imprisonment or death, was justified if it brought glory to God. What an attitude!

LIVING COMMENTARY NOTE:

Many Christians are so full of self-love that it wouldn't matter if their imprisonment had furthered the Gospel. All they would be focused on was the fact that they were suffering. They would care more about what's happening to them than the kingdom of God. And that's precisely why they aren't having the impact that Paul had.

Self-love is a huge obstacle to God working His will through us. All those who will live godly shall suffer persecution (2 Tim. 3:12). If we love ourselves inordinately, our self-love will always compel us to compromise and stop what is best for the kingdom from coming to pass.

Here and in the next few verses, the Apostle Paul gave a wonderful example of a person who had died to himself and was living only for the One who had died for him.

DISCIPLESHIP QUESTIONS

1. *Discussion question:* What does it mean to you to be focused on your own suffering even if that suffering futhered the Gospel?

2. What was Paul's attitude?

So that my bonds in Christ are manifest in all the palace, and in all other places;

PHILIPPIANS 1:13

LIFE FOR TODAY STUDY BIBLE NOTES:

• As a result of Paul's imprisonment, all the soldiers of the emperor's house were exposed to the Gospel of Christ. The phrase **"all other places"** reveals that the general public was also aware of Paul's situation and had come into contact with the claims of Christianity through it.

LIVING COMMENTARY NOTE:

Even though Paul was suffering imprisonment, he was saying it was worth it all because everyone in the caesar's palace had heard the Gospel. Paul was very outspoken about his faith. Many Christians today wouldn't care about whether or not others were blessed because of their hardships. They would be focused on themselves, and that's the very reason they wouldn't have the results that Paul had here.

DISCIPLESHIP QUESTIONS

1. *Discussion question:* Paul didn't let being in prison stop him from sharing the Gospel. What can you learn from his example?

And many of the brethren in the Lord, waxing confident by my bonds, are much more bold to speak the word without fear.

PHILIPPIANS 1:14

LIFE FOR TODAY STUDY BIBLE NOTES:

• Paul's uncompromising stand and the way that it was furthering the Gospel had encouraged others to be bolder in their presentation of the Gospel. Anytime we show strength in the face of adversity, the Lord uses that to motivate others to achieve the same level of commitment. Courage inspires courage.

LIVING COMMENTARY NOTE:

Paul's suffering inspired other ministers to become bolder in their presentation of the Gospel.

DISCIPLESHIP QUESTIONS

1. Paul's suffering inspired other ministers to become _____ in their presentation of the Gospel.

2. *Discussion question:* Why do you think that courage inspires courage?

Some indeed preach Christ even of envy and strife; and some also of good will:

PHILIPPIANS 1:15

LIFE FOR TODAY
STUDY BIBLE NOTES:

• Two totally different motives were spoken of here. Some people ministered out of envy and strife—that is, from a jealous and quarrelsome spirit (see my note at Phil. 1:16)—while others ministered from pure motives, right intentions, and good will. Today, as in Paul's day, the preaching of Christ is done both out of love for the Lord and also out of contention and insincerity. Whether the Word is preached from good motivation or bad, the Word is what "works"—not the messenger. Therefore, we can rejoice that Christ is being preached even when wrong motives are behind it.

DISCIPLESHIP QUESTIONS

1. What two motives were behind the preaching of Christ?

2. *Discussion question:* What do you think it means for people to preach out of contention and insincerity?

3. Why can you rejoice that Christ is being preached even when wrong motives are behind it?

The one preach Christ of contention, not sincerely, supposing to add affliction to my bonds:

PHILIPPIANS 1:16

LIFE FOR TODAY STUDY BIBLE NOTES:

• What was Paul referring to? How can a person motivated by contention and insincerity preach Christ? How could that have added affliction to the imprisonment Paul was already suffering?

This is probably referring to people who had heard the claims Paul made about Jesus being raised from the dead but didn't believe him. As they repeated these details to others in mockery, the Gospel of Jesus' death, burial, and resurrection was spreading, and the Holy Spirit could use that. Regardless of the motives, the Truth was spreading. Paul was rejoicing that people were being exposed to the claims of Christianity.

LIVING COMMENTARY NOTE:

This passage is a little hard to understand. I don't think Paul was rejoicing about fellow Christians who were preaching Christ from the wrong motive, seeking to make his affliction even worse. I think he was talking about unbelievers who had heard that a prisoner in custody was preaching that a man named Jesus died for man's sins and rose the third day. These unbelievers didn't believe what they were talking about. They were just repeating in mockery what they had heard, thinking their insult would make Paul's affliction even worse. But nonetheless, Paul was rejoicing because the news of a Savior who died and rose again for man's salvation was being proclaimed. The Holy Spirit could work with that.

DISCIPLESHIP QUESTIONS

1. *Discussion question:* Why or why not do you agree with Andrew's interpretation of this verse?

But the other of love, knowing that I am set for the defence of the gospel.

PHILIPPIANS 1:17

LIFE FOR TODAY STUDY BIBLE NOTES:

- Many true believers were inspired by Paul's faithfulness in the face of persecution, and they had become even bolder in their presentation of the Gospel. Paul's obvious love for the Lord had caused them to love God more and to love the Apostle Paul also for his selfless example. All this advanced the Gospel.

LIVING COMMENTARY NOTE:

This is speaking of the true ministers of the Lord Jesus Christ who were inspired to be bolder because of the testimony of Paul and his steadfastness in the face of persecution.

DISCIPLESHIP QUESTIONS

1. Why were true ministers of the Lord Jesus Christ inspired to be bolder?

2. *Discussion question*: How are those who are being persecuted for their faith an inspiration to you and others?

What then? notwithstanding, every way, whether in pretence, or in truth, Christ is preached; and I therein do rejoice, yea, and will rejoice.

PHILIPPIANS 1:18

LIFE FOR TODAY STUDY BIBLE NOTES:

• If Christ was being talked about to people who had never heard of Him before, Paul found reason to rejoice. Paul didn't care about himself. He was single in his focus of the advancement of the kingdom. People couldn't believe on Jesus if they hadn't heard of Him and what He had accomplished (Rom. 10:17). So, regardless of the motive, Paul rejoiced that the details of Christ's death and resurrection were being proclaimed.

LIVING COMMENTARY NOTE:

Paul didn't care if those who were talking about Jesus were mocking him or inspired by him. If Jesus was being glorified, then he was blessed. What a great attitude. It wasn't all about Paul. Paul's focus was only on glorifying Jesus. That's the reason we are still speaking of him 2,000 years later.

DISCIPLESHIP QUESTIONS

1. According to this verse, what was Paul's reaction to people preaching Christ, whether in **"pretence"** or **"truth"**?

2. Was Paul's focus on himself?

For I know that this shall turn to my salvation through your prayer, and the supply of the Spirit of Jesus Christ,

PHILIPPIANS 1:19

LIFE FOR TODAY STUDY BIBLE NOTES:

- The word **"salvation"** was translated from the Greek word *soteria*, and this Greek word means "rescue or safety" (*Strong's Concordance*). It can be referring to either physical or spiritual salvation. Therefore, some people have interpreted Paul's statements here to mean that he was predicting his release from jail. Yet, in the very next verse (which is still the same sentence), Paul stated that he didn't know if the outcome of his imprisonment would be life or death. That would lead us to believe that Paul was speaking of his eternal salvation in this verse and not a temporal deliverance from prison.

The Scriptures teach that rewards are given to those who endure persecution for the Gospel's sake. Paul was saying that he would be rewarded for his stand for the Gospel and the impact he was making whether the listeners mocked him or emulated him.

LIVING COMMENTARY NOTE:

Even the ridicule and persecution we receive will work to our advantage. In eternity, the Lord will more than compensate us for whatever injustice or injury we sustained because of our faithfulness to Him. What a deal!

DISCIPLESHIP QUESTIONS

1. Can the ridicule and persecution you receive work to your advantage?

2. What will the Lord do for you in eternity?

3. What does *soteria* mean?

4. *Discussion question:* What do the words **"salvation"** and *soteria* mean to you?

According to my earnest expectation and my hope, that in nothing I shall be ashamed, but that with all boldness, as always, so now also Christ shall be magnified in my body, whether it be by life, or by death.

PHILIPPIANS 1:20

LIFE FOR TODAY STUDY BIBLE NOTES:

- Paul didn't just hope that he would glorify the Lord with his actions; he had an earnest expectation and hope. The difference between excellence and mediocrity is often not what is believed but the degree to which something is believed. Paul was fully persuaded (Rom. 4:21).

- This wasn't the first time Paul had been bold. He was expressing his earnest expectation and hope that he would again be bold in the face of death, like he always had been. One of the reasons people fold under pressure is because they wait until the "big" situations to believe God. If they have not learned to trust God in the small things, they will not be able to trust Him in the big things.

When David fought Goliath (1 Sam. 17), everyone mocked him because of his belief that he could win. Goliath was a giant, and David was only a small boy. But David said something very important in his defense. In 1 Samuel 17:34-37, David revealed that this was not the first time he had depended on God for a victory against something bigger than himself. Before facing Goliath, he had killed a lion and a bear with his bare hands. He **knew** he could defeat Goliath with God's help.

Paul could be confident of the outcome of his actions, regardless of the cost, because he had put his faith to the test many times before. Paul had lived a life of boldness for many years. Faith must be developed, much like a muscle. Those who wait until the day of the contest to start training are going to lose. That's not the way it works in the natural or in the spiritual.

LIVING COMMENTARY NOTE:

Paul's sole desire was for Jesus to be glorified. If his death would glorify God, then so be it. What a great attitude! We should all be like-minded.

Just like Proverbs 10:28 and 11:7, Paul used the word **"expectation"** to describe hope. See Romans 8:24.

PHILIPPIANS 1:20 *(Continued)*

LIFE FOR TODAY
STUDY BIBLE NOTES:

• Many people are committed to the Lord and the furtherance of His kingdom, because they trust they will come out on top with Him. However, very few people are committed to the Lord when it begins to cost them personally. Paul's commitment was the same whether the personal results were life or death. Paul had died to himself. You can't kill a dead man.

DISCIPLESHIP QUESTIONS

1. If people have not learned to trust God in the _____ things, they will not be able to trust Him in the _____ things.

2. What gave Paul confidence in the outcome of his actions?

3. *Discussion question:* What are some ways that you can exercise your faith like a muscle and develop it?

4. Very few people are committed to the Lord when what happens?

For to me to live is Christ, and to die is gain.

PHILIPPIANS 1:21

LIFE FOR TODAY STUDY BIBLE NOTES:

• What is life all about? What is the purpose of one's existence? What is to be gained in life? What do people live for? Paul answered these questions by saying that the process of life and continuous living is only to be found in Christ. Paul indicated that true life is only to be found in Christ. It is not to be found in prestige, fortune, fame, or things, but only in the one who is life—Jesus Christ (John 14:6; 1 John 1:1-2, 5:12, and 20). This life is a quality of life, not a quantity of time. God has given us eternal life, and this life is in His Son (1 John 5:11).

When we say so-and-so is "my life," we mean that all of our attention is given to, our focus is directed toward, and our purpose in living revolves around that person. In a similar way, Paul's sole purpose was to be totally consumed with Christ and His life. To Paul, life was Christ. We should have the same attitude.

• The word *gain* means to advance or progress. Many people do not have this perspective that death is better than life. Those who are not born again go directly into eternal torment, but for those who are born again (John 3:3), death is the doorway that brings them into the very presence of God. Death is promotion for the saint.

Fear of death causes people to compromise their convictions and brings them into bondage (Heb. 2:15). Understanding that death ushers the believer into an existence that is infinitely better than life here on earth breaks all fear and allows believers to act as instructed by the Lord, regardless of the consequences. Death is not the

LIVING COMMENTARY NOTE:

What a radical statement. To a lost person, this would be ludicrous. But for the Christian, this is truth, though not all Christians think this way. If our physical lives here on earth continue, our focus should be Christ and what He has done for us, not things. And if our earthly existences end, our heavenly existences begin. The glories prepared for us in heaven are infinitely greater than any benefit we could ever have here on earth. There is no comparison (Rom. 8:18).

This attitude should not be limited to the Apostle Paul or a few "super-saints." This should be the mindset of all true believers. Not understanding this truth is at the root of all fear. If we have died to our own lives and are only letting Christ live through us, then there is nothing to fear. If we live, Christ will love us and use us. If we die, it will only get better. We can't lose for winning.

PHILIPPIANS 1:21 *(Continued)*

LIFE FOR TODAY
STUDY BIBLE NOTES:

end; it is just the beginning for those who put their faith in Christ.

DISCIPLESHIP QUESTIONS

1. If you have died to your own life and are only letting Christ live through you, then what?

2. *Discussion question:* How can meditating on this verse and letting it become part of your thinking affect your life?

3. This life is a _____ of life, not a quantity of _____.

4. What is death for the saint?

5. What does fear of death do to people?

But if I live in the flesh, this is the fruit of my labour: yet what I shall choose I wot not.

PHILIPPIANS 1:22

LIFE FOR TODAY STUDY BIBLE NOTES:

• The *New International Version* translated this verse as **"If I am to go on living in the body, this will mean fruitful labor for me."** Other translations follow the same thought. However, it seems clearer and more in line with the context to interpret it differently.

Paul had been speaking of his imprisonment throughout this chapter. He was saying, "My present circumstances (imprisonment) are the result of my life in the flesh, yet I am torn between two choices. I desire to depart and be with Christ, which is best for me, but it is more beneficial for you for me to stay here with you."

Despite the fact that Paul suffered more than most (1 Cor. 4:9 and 2 Cor. 12:7), he was willing to bear that pain for the sake of others.

• **"I wot not"** is an old English phrase for "I don't know." Paul was having trouble deciding between life and death. Not many people struggle with that choice. Many of those who long for death are not doing so because of a desire to be with Christ but because of a desire to escape some hardship in this life. Paul was different. He had such a vibrant relationship with Christ that he had to use his faith to stay in his physical body.

This was one reason Paul was so bold and effective. No one could intimidate or scare him. Paul had already resolved the issue of death. He wasn't afraid to die; he was looking forward to it. This made him fearless and focused. We should be like him.

LIVING COMMENTARY NOTE:

Paul had just said that living in this physical body was awesome and dying was even better. Here, he said that living in his physical body meant imprisonment and suffering. Yet, he couldn't decide what was better. Most would say being with Christ in glory would be better. But Paul didn't evaluate things on the basis of what would benefit him the most. He had died to self and was alive to God and others more than self. Thus, he concluded that he would choose to stay in the body so that he could be of benefit to others.

This is one of the main reasons very few have affected their world the way Paul affected his. We are too self-centered. If following the Lord costs us too much, we often choose not to follow. This has decreased our effectiveness. In contrast, Paul didn't value his life so highly, and therefore, Christ could live through him however He chose.

PHILIPPIANS 1:22 *(Continued)*

DISCIPLESHIP QUESTIONS

1. What was Paul's reason for choosing to stay in the body?

2. *Discussion question:* What are some of the ways that Paul's attitude affected his life and outlook, despite his being in prison?

For I am in a strait betwixt two, having a desire to depart, and to be with Christ; which is far better:

PHILIPPIANS 1:23

LIFE FOR TODAY STUDY BIBLE NOTES:

- Paul was pulled in two directions: desiring to leave this life and be with Christ, and desiring to remain alive for the sake of the saints. In Philippians 1:25, he revealed his choice. He chose to stay in this life so that others might progress in the furtherance and joy of their faith. Paul's staying caused many to glorify Christ for Paul's safety and his visit to them again.

- Paul's way of thinking here is not the most common way of viewing things, even among Christians, but this really is impeccable logic. If we seriously thought about what the Scriptures teach us about our life with Christ after this physical life, we would all think like Paul. The things prepared for us (John 14:2-3) are so wonderful that we can't totally comprehend them with our finite minds (1 John 3:1). We need to value our eternal lives more and our temporal lives less. This would solve many problems and remove a lot of grief.

LIVING COMMENTARY NOTE:

Paul was in a strait because he longed to be in heaven with Christ but felt it necessary to remain in the physical body for the sake of others. Most people are in a strait because they don't have this attitude. They love themselves so much that they are addicted to fulfilling their every lust and get perplexed when every whim isn't met.

DISCIPLESHIP QUESTIONS

1. Why was Paul in a strait?

2. Why are most people in a strait?

3. You would think like Paul if you did what?

4. *Discussion question:* What steps, if any, do you feel you need to take to value your eternal life more and your temporal life less?

Nevertheless to abide in the flesh is more needful for you.

PHILIPPIANS 1:24

LIFE FOR TODAY STUDY BIBLE NOTES:

• Paul had a vision of heaven that made him long to go there, yet he was remaining in his physical body for the sake of others. Most people are clinging to this physical life for selfish reasons. Paul was clinging to it for totally unselfish reasons. Only when people lose their lives (die to self and live for Christ and others) do they truly find out what life is all about (Matt. 10:39).

LIVING COMMENTARY NOTE:

Sadly, there are people without whom the world would be better off. Paul wasn't one of those people. Paul's life made a positive difference in the lives of many people.

DISCIPLESHIP QUESTIONS

1. **"Nevertheless to _____ in the flesh is more needful for _____."**

2. *Discussion question:* What are some of the ways that losing your life (dying to self and living for Christ and others) can show you what life is all about?

And having this confidence, I know that I shall abide and continue with you all for your furtherance and joy of faith;

PHILIPPIANS 1:25

LIFE FOR TODAY STUDY BIBLE NOTES:

• The way Paul spoke in these verses indicates that he had the power to choose whether he lived or died. This has to be understood in light of the scripture that says, **"It is appointed unto men once to die"** (Heb. 9:27). No one lives forever unless he or she is among those who remain at the second coming of the Lord. However, through faith, believers can prolong their days on the earth or shorten them through unbelief.

LIVING COMMENTARY NOTE:

Paul was committed to glorifying God, whether by his life or death. But he was confident that living would bring more glory to the Lord than his death, and therefore, he was certain he would be released. He didn't evaluate things on the basis of physical things but knew spiritual truth dominated physical things.

DISCIPLESHIP QUESTIONS

1. What was Paul confident about?

2. *Discussion question:* How do you think you can prolong your days on this earth through faith or shorten them through unbelief?

That your rejoicing may be more abundant in Jesus Christ for me by my coming to you again.

PHILIPPIANS 1:26

LIFE FOR TODAY STUDY BIBLE NOTES:

- Paul knew that his return to Philippi would bring joy and rejoicing to the saints there. That's awesome! Paul didn't have some false humility that made him see himself as a worm. He knew that he was nothing in himself, but he also knew who he was in the Lord and that God's power in him made him someone these Philippians loved and longed to see again.

LIVING COMMENTARY NOTE:

Paul knew the Philippians would rejoice greatly to see him come to them again. There was a lot of love between them. Lord, let me impact people in such a positive way that there would be those who would long to see me come to them and they would rejoice.

DISCIPLESHIP QUESTIONS

1. Would the Philippians chase Paul away if he came to them again?

2. *Discussion question:* Why or why not are you willing to make Andrew's prayer—"Lord, let me impact people in such a positive way that there would be those who would long to see me come to them and they would rejoice"—your own?

3. What made Paul someone that the Philippians loved and longed to see again?

Only let your conversation be as it becometh the gospel of Christ: that whether I come and see you, or else be absent, I may hear of your affairs, that ye stand fast in one spirit, with one mind striving together for the faith of the gospel;

PHILIPPIANS 1:27

LIFE FOR TODAY STUDY BIBLE NOTES:

- The *New King James Version* translated this phrase—**"let your conversation be as it becometh the gospel of Christ"**—as **"let your conduct be worthy of the gospel of Christ."** The word **"conversation,"** as used in the *King James Version*, always refers to behavior, conduct, or a manner of life. In the Greek text, **"conversation"** is conveyed as a present imperative. That means Paul was giving a command concerning habit and lifestyle. Paul was promoting godly living that will glorify the Gospel of Christ. Grace is the only proper motivation for living a truly godly life.

- As Paul discussed holy living (see the previous *Life for Today* note at this verse), he turned to one of his favorite themes: unity among the believers (1 Cor. 1:10). Jesus said this is the greatest witness we can give the world (John 13:35). Other acts of holiness are minor compared to loving the brethren. Those of us who focus on moral acts of holiness more than loving our brethren are missing the mark. If we can't love our brother whom we have seen, how can we expect to love God whom we cannot see (1 John 4:20)?

LIVING COMMENTARY NOTE:

Paul didn't just exhort the Philippians individually to strive for the faith of the Gospel; he specifically exhorted them to strive together collectively with one mind for the faith of the Gospel. I believe there are some things the Lord wants to accomplish that cannot be accomplished on just an individual level. There has to be unity in the body of Christ.

DISCIPLESHIP QUESTIONS

1. Why does there need to be unity in the body of Christ?

2. What does **"conversation"** in the *King James Version* always refer to?

3. In the Greek text, **"conversation"** was given in the present imperative. What does this mean?

4. *Discussion question:* Jesus said the greatest witness you can give the world is unity among the believers (John 13:35 and 1 Cor. 1:10). Why do you think that is?

And in nothing terrified by your adversaries: which is to them an evident token of perdition, but to you of salvation, and that of God.

PHILIPPIANS 1:28

LIFE FOR TODAY STUDY BIBLE NOTES:

• The word **"terrified"** in the Greek is a strong term referring to the shying away of a horse that has been startled. The **"adversaries"** who caused this fear were unbelievers who showed hatred and hostility to the Philippian believers. So, Paul was speaking of persecution against the Philippian believers. The persecution these adversaries brought against the Philippians was a token that the persecutors were headed for perdition. If they were true believers, they would not be fighting their own.

On the other hand, to those who are the persecuted, persecution is a token that they are truly born again. Jesus taught that godly people would be persecuted (Matt. 5:10-12), and so did Paul (2 Tim. 3:12). The fact that these believers were being persecuted confirmed their salvation and, at the same time, revealed their persecutors as being enemies of Christ with the result of eternal perdition.

The suffering of persecution is not an indication of divine disapproval but rather a sign of true adoption into the family of God. We are called not only to believe in Christ but also to suffer for His sake (Phil. 1:29). The Philippians were experiencing the same type of persecution that Paul was going through (Phil. 1:30). Paul was stating to the Philippian believers that they were in this fight together and should therefore receive encouragement and strength from each other.

LIVING COMMENTARY NOTE:

It is a little unclear to me what this verse is saying. It is either saying that our fearlessness in the face of persecution makes the unbelievers think of us as beyond hope, or our fearlessness shows us both the perdition of the unbelievers and our certainty of salvation.

PHILIPPIANS 1:28 *(Continued)*

DISCIPLESHIP QUESTIONS

1. *Discussion question:* What do you think this verse is saying?

2. What did the persecution against the Philippians do?

3. What is the suffering of persecution, and what is it not?

For unto you it is given in the behalf of Christ, not only to believe on him, but also to suffer for his sake;

PHILIPPIANS 1:29

LIFE FOR TODAY STUDY BIBLE NOTES:

• Suffering persecution is not just for missionaries in foreign lands. Second Timothy 3:12 says, **"Yea, and all that will live godly in Christ Jesus shall suffer persecution."** All Christians who live godly lives will be persecuted. The only Christians who are not persecuted are those who are not living godly lives.

True Christianity is exactly opposite of the whole world system. We are headed in a selfless direction, while the world is consumed with self. Jesus teaches us to love, while the world is full of hate. We are supposed to turn the other cheek, while the world takes this as another opportunity to hurt us. The world and Christianity are in conflict. The only reason any of us would not suffer persecution is if we were headed in the same direction as the unbelievers. When we go God's way, we will bump into the devil.

Persecution isn't always life threatening or physically abusive. Some of the most subtle persecution is just rejection or mockery.

LIVING COMMENTARY NOTE:

This is the same truth Paul presented in 2 Timothy 3:12 – **"Yea, and all that will live godly in Christ Jesus shall suffer persecution."** This is a part of the Christian life. The only people who don't experience persecution are ungodly people. If we are headed the same direction as the devil, we don't cross paths often. But when we turn and start swimming upstream, against the flow, there will be much more opposition.

DISCIPLESHIP QUESTIONS

1. *Discussion question:* What do you think it means to be persecuted?

2. *Discussion question:* Do you agree with the statement "The only people who don't experience persecution are ungodly people"? Why or why not?

3. When you go _____ way, you will bump into the _____.

Having the same conflict which ye saw in me, and now hear to be in me.

PHILIPPIANS 1:30

LIFE FOR TODAY STUDY BIBLE NOTES:

• The Philippians had come under persecution just like Paul. They had seen Paul and Silas thrown in jail (Acts 16:23) on their first visit to Philippi, and they had heard how Paul had been imprisoned in Jerusalem (Acts 21:33) and then sent to Rome (Acts 25:11). Here they were, experiencing persecution as well.

LIVING COMMENTARY NOTE:

Paul was in prison. He was saying here that the sufferings he had endured were not limited to him but all Christians (who live godly lives [2 Tim. 3:12]) will suffer persecution.

DISCIPLESHIP QUESTIONS

1. Were the sufferings Paul endured limited to him?

2. *Discussion question:* In what ways do you think believers are persecuted today?

PHILIPPIANS 1
Answer Key

PHILIPPIANS 1:1

1. They were beaten and thrown in jail, and sang praises to God at midnight in the dungeon (Acts 16:22-25). The Lord sent an earthquake that broke all the prisoners' chains and opened their cell doors, but none of them escaped (Acts 16:26-28). The jailer received salvation as a result (Acts 16:30-33)

2. As a slave of Jesus Christ

3. *Discussion question*

4. *Discussion question*

PHILIPPIANS 1:2

1. God the Father and the Lord Jesus Christ

2. **"Justified by faith"**

3. Through being reconciled to God by grace

4. *Discussion question*

PHILIPPIANS 1:3

1. The Philippians were Paul's partners

2. *Discussion question*

PHILIPPIANS 1:4

1. He remembered the Philippians and prayed for them every time he prayed

2. *Discussion question*

PHILIPPIANS 1:5

1. They supported him financially after he left their area

2. *Discussion question*

PHILIPPIANS 1:6

1. People who are partners, who are not just takers but have moved into the realm of givers
2. No
3. The second coming of Christ

PHILIPPIANS 1:7

1. *Discussion question*

PHILIPPIANS 1:8

1. *Discussion question*
2. Motives / important
3. The seat of the affections; i.e., your emotions

PHILIPPIANS 1:9

1. How much you know and discern God's love for you
2. **"Hath" / "all things" / "knowledge"**
3. The more your love for God and others will abound
4. *Discussion question*

PHILIPPIANS 1:10

1. Perfecting God's love in them
2. *Discussion question*

PHILIPPIANS 1:11

1. More fruit of righteousness

PHILIPPIANS 1:12

1. *Discussion question*
2. His heart and focus were so fixed on God that any price he had to pay, even imprisonment or death, was justified if it brought glory to God

PHILIPPIANS 1:13

1. *Discussion question*

PHILIPPIANS 1:14

1. Bolder

2. *Discussion question*

PHILIPPIANS 1:15

1. Envy and strife (that is, from a jealous and quarrelsome spirit), and pure motives, right intentions, and good will

2. *Discussion question*

3. Because it is the Word that "works"—not the messenger

PHILIPPIANS 1:16

1. *Discussion question*

PHILIPPIANS 1:17

1. Because of the testimony of Paul and his steadfastness in the face of persecution

2. *Discussion question*

PHILIPPIANS 1:18

1. He rejoiced

2. No

PHILIPPIANS 1:19

1. Yes

2. More than compensate you for whatever injustice or injury you sustained because of your faithfulness to Him

3. "Rescue or safety"

4. *Discussion question*

PHILIPPIANS 1:20

1. Small / big
2. He had put his faith to the test many times before
3. *Discussion question*
4. When it begins to cost them personally

PHILIPPIANS 1:21

1. There is nothing to fear
2. *Discussion question*
3. Quality / time
4. A promotion
5. It causes them to compromise their convictions and brings them into bondage

PHILIPPIANS 1:22

1. So he could be a benefit to others
2. *Discussion question*

PHILIPPIANS 1:23

1. Because he longed to be in heaven with Christ but felt it necessary to remain in the physical body for the sake of others
2. Because they don't have this attitude—they love themselves so much that they are addicted to fulfilling every lust and get perplexed when every whim isn't met
3. If you seriously thought about what the Scriptures teach you about your life with Christ after this physical life
4. *Discussion question*

PHILIPPIANS 1:24

1. **"Abide" / "you"**
2. *Discussion question*

PHILIPPIANS 1:25

1. That living would bring more glory to the Lord than his death, and therefore, he was certain he would be released

2. *Discussion question*

PHILIPPIANS 1:26

1. No, they would rejoice greatly to see him

2. *Discussion question*

3. God's power in him

PHILIPPIANS 1:27

1. Because there are some things the Lord wants to accomplish that cannot be accomplished on just an individual level

2. Behavior, conduct, or a manner of life

3. It is a command concerning habit and lifestyle

4. *Discussion question*

PHILIPPIANS 1:28

1. *Discussion question*

2. It confirmed their salvation and revealed their persecutors as being enemies of Christ with the result of eternal perdition

3. It is not an indication of divine disapproval but rather a sign of true adoption into the family of God

PHILIPPIANS 1:29

1. *Discussion question*

2. *Discussion question*

3. God's / devil

PHILIPPIANS 1:30

1. No

2. *Discussion question*

PHILIPPIANS 2

If there be therefore any consolation in Christ, if any comfort of love, if any fellowship of the Spirit, if any bowels and mercies,

PHILIPPIANS 2:1

LIFE FOR TODAY STUDY BIBLE NOTES:

- The word **"if"** is used four times in this verse, but these are not really four questions. In the Greek, these clauses do not covey doubt but are used for emphasis. The "ifs" could have been translated "since." **Since** there is consolation in Christ, **since** His love comforts us, **since** we have fellowship with Him through the Spirit, and **since** our hearts are full of His mercy. Since the Lord has done all these things for us, we should love our fellow believers (Phil. 2:2). If God could love us, then we should love each other.

- The word **"consolation"** means "a comfort" (*American Heritage Dictionary*). The *New International Version* translated this word as **"encouragement."** It is a major understatement to say that we are comforted and encouraged through Christ.

LIVING COMMENTARY NOTE:

Of course there are all of these things in abundance in the Lord. Therefore, Paul was telling the Philippians that since what God offers is so much more in quantity and quality than anything the world has to offer, they should value their lives in Christ more than this physical life and this physical world.

DISCIPLESHIP QUESTIONS

1. According to Paul, why were the Philippians to value their lives in Christ more than this physical life and this physical world?

2. *Discussion question:* How are you comforted and encouraged through Christ?

Fulfil ye my joy, that ye be likeminded, having the same love, being of one accord, of one mind.

PHILIPPIANS 2:2

LIFE FOR TODAY STUDY BIBLE NOTES:

- Of course the answer to all the "ifs" in this verse is a resounding yes! There is consolation and comfort of love in Christ, there is an awesome fellowship with the Holy Spirit, and tremendous mercies have been bestowed on us through Christ. Therefore, Paul was using the marvelous blessings given unto us as motivation for us giving back to God. What Paul encouraged us to give to the Lord is a humble heart in our dealings with other believers, resulting in unity.

- Paul's joy was the unity of the body of Christ. Many Christians don't find any joy in seeing the members of Christ's body in unity. In fact, many people don't believe this is possible. However, it is possible, and the goal of every Christian should be to walk in love with the brethren.

- The unity Paul was speaking of is much deeper than what most of us today can believe or comprehend (see 1 Cor. 1:10). He was speaking of being of one accord and one mind. This means we are to think the same way. How can that happen? Paul went on to explain that it happens through humility. Pride is at the root of all division (Prov. 13:10). Until pride is dealt with, there will be no true unity. As long as pride is prevalent, division will be too.

LIVING COMMENTARY NOTE:

Paul wasn't just admonishing the Philippians to be likeminded with each other; he was telling them to have the same mind that he had concerning not seeking their own welfare but, rather, the welfare of the kingdom. He said in Philippians 1:21, **"For to me to live is Christ, and to die is gain."** That's the unselfish attitude he was instructing the Philippians to adopt.

DISCIPLESHIP QUESTIONS

1. What should be the goal of every Christian?

2. What prevents true unity?

3. *Discussion question:* How do you think you can help promote unity in the body of Christ?

Let nothing be done through strife or vainglory; but in lowliness of mind let each esteem other better than themselves.

PHILIPPIANS 2:3

LIFE FOR TODAY STUDY BIBLE NOTES:

• Humility can be defined in many ways, one of which is the absence of pride. Typically, pride is described as arrogance, but that is just one dimension of pride. Timidness is also pride, because, in its simplest terms, pride is self-centeredness and a timid or shy person is very self-centered. Paul gave the antidote to self-centeredness here: esteeming others better than oneself.

• How can we esteem others better than ourselves when, in truth, we really think we are better than others? Some people are better athletes than others, some are better businesspeople than others, some are better speakers than others, and so forth.

First, we need to recognize that our accomplishments don't make us better than others. There is a difference between what we do and who we are. Better performance does not make better people. People's character can be severely wanting even though their performance is good. A classic example of this is found in the Pharisees of Jesus' day. They did the right things for all the wrong reasons. Inside they were corrupt. Our evaluation of others needs to change. God judges by looking on the inside, not the outside (1 Sam. 16:7). We need to esteem others on this same basis.

Second, to esteem others better than ourselves simply means to value them more than we value ourselves. To some, that may seem impossible, but it isn't. That is exactly what Jesus did, and Paul used Jesus as the model for what he was preaching here in the next few verses (Phil. 2:5-11). If Jesus, who was God in the flesh (1 Tim. 3:16), could

LIVING COMMENTARY NOTE:

Paul revealed that the antidote to strife is lowliness of mind, or considering others better than ourselves. Indeed, **"only by pride cometh contention"** (Prov. 13:10). People cannot be in strife without being prideful, and they cannot be prideful without being in strife.

In the previous chapter, Paul had said that death ushered us into the presence of Christ and was therefore better than physical life (Phil. 1:21-23). But he was willing to deny his own needs so that he could be a channel of God's supply to others. In other words, Paul was saying we should live our lives for others and not for ourselves. He had used himself as an example of this selfless life. And he pointed their attention to Jesus as the supreme example of a selfless life.

PHILIPPIANS 2:3 *(Continued)*

LIFE FOR TODAY
STUDY BIBLE NOTES:

humble Himself and value the good of others above His own welfare, then we should certainly be able to do the same. It can happen when we die to self and live to God (Rom. 6:2).

DISCIPLESHIP QUESTIONS

1. **"Let nothing be done through _____ or vainglory; but in lowliness of mind let each _____ other better than _____."**

2. What is the antidote to strife?

3. Who is your supreme example of a selfless life?

4. *Discussion question:* Do you feel you demonstrate pride more as arrogance or as timidity? What can you do to walk in humility more?

5. *Discussion question:* Do you recognize that your accomplishments don't make you better than others? What are some scriptures you can meditate on to help you see that what you do is different from who you are?

Look not every man on his own things, but every man also on the things of others.

PHILIPPIANS 2:4

LIFE FOR TODAY STUDY BIBLE NOTES:

- The way we implement the instruction of the previous verse to esteem others better than ourselves is to look at their side of things instead of seeing everything through selfish eyes. If we think only about ourselves, we will be selfish. If we get out of self and think more about the benefit of others than the benefit of self, then we will be selfless. It's a matter of focus. Whichever side of things we focus on is the side we will take. Therefore, **"look not every man on his own things, but every man also on the things of others."**

LIVING COMMENTARY NOTE:

This isn't telling us to be busybodies or nosy. It's just saying we should look at things from the other person's perspective too.

DISCIPLESHIP QUESTIONS

1. Is this verse telling you to be a busybody or nosey?

2. *Discussion question:* Have you made it a habit to look at things from the other side instead of seeing everything through selfish eyes? How has this impacted your life?

3. *Discussion question:* What changes do you think would be made if believers got out of self and thought more about the benefit of others?

Let this mind be in you, which was also in Christ Jesus:

PHILIPPIANS 2:5

LIFE FOR TODAY STUDY BIBLE NOTES:

- The understood subject of this sentence is the word "you." Paul was saying, "You let this mind be in you." Through the new birth, the Lord has given us the mind of Christ (1 Cor. 2:16), but it is still our choice to let this mind function in us.

- The phrase **"let this mind"** (*King James Version*) or **"have this attitude"** (*New American Standard Version*) is in the present imperative; that means it carries the idea of a commitment or a way of doing something as a lifestyle or a general habit. It primarily denotes a state of mind and an inward attitude rather than an act of thinking. Paul was speaking here about a heart attitude expressed as a lifestyle.

- We are seeing an insight into the mind of the Lord Jesus Christ Himself described in Philippians 2:5-8. Jesus was God manifest in the flesh, and He certainly would have been justified in being arrogant. Yet, He was just the opposite. Paul was drawing on the attitude that Jesus displayed toward us, in order to encourage us to treat others with the same selfless love. The *New International Version* says, **"Your attitude should be the same as that of Christ Jesus."**

LIVING COMMENTARY NOTE:

Jesus is the supreme example of looking at things from the other person's point of view. Jesus took the form of flesh so that He could know exactly how we feel. He gave up everything so He could identify with us. What an example.

DISCIPLESHIP QUESTIONS

1. What makes Jesus the supreme example of looking at things from the other person's point of view?

2. *Discussion question*: In what areas of your life do you think your attitude could be more like Christ's? What will you do to accomplish that goal?

Who, being in the form of God, thought it not robbery to be equal with God:

PHILIPPIANS 2:6

LIFE FOR TODAY STUDY BIBLE NOTES:

• Jesus in His preexistent state was in the form of God. **"In the beginning was the Word, and the Word was with God, and the Word was God"** (John 1:1). The Greek word *morphe* was translated **"form"** here in Philippians 2:6. This Greek word means "the nature or essence" (*Vine's Expository Dictionary*). Jesus was God manifest in the flesh (1 Tim. 3:16).

However, Jesus did not demand or cling to His rights as God. He laid aside His divine rights and privileges in order to take the form of a servant and be made in the likeness of man. He further humbled Himself by becoming obedient to the Father, even to the point of death.

This was the supreme sacrifice that identified Jesus totally with humanity and enabled God to redeem mankind. By dying a criminal's death upon the cross, Jesus fulfilled the Old Testament prophecy in Deuteronomy 21:23 and bore our curse in His own body. This redeemed us from that curse and opened wide God's blessing of justification through faith in Christ and the promise of His Holy Spirit (Gal. 3:13-14).

• Paul was saying that Jesus did not think it was unjust to be equal with God. The reason He thought that way was because, in truth, He **was** equal with God. Jesus is God. This is a very clear reference to the deity of Jesus.

It is unfortunate that the *New International Version* translated this verse as **"Who, being in very nature God, did not consider equality with God something to be grasped."** This leaves the

LIVING COMMENTARY NOTE:

I really dislike the *New International Version* translation of this verse: **"Who, being in very nature God, did not consider equality with God something to be grasped."** It makes this very clear passage unclear. This verse is simply saying that Jesus didn't think equality with God was wrong to claim for Himself. It was absolutely true. He was God and was therefore totally equal to God. But He laid all of His divinity and glory aside and took upon Himself the form of a man.

LIFE FOR TODAY STUDY BIBLE NOTES:

impression that Jesus wasn't divine, and the *NIV Study Bible* presents that as one interpretation of this verse. Yet the first part of the verse, even in the *NIV*, says Jesus was **"in very nature God."**

The Message translated this verse as **"He had equal status with God but didn't think so much of himself that he had to cling to the advantages of that status no matter what."** The whole point of Paul's statements is to show how much Jesus humbled Himself for our sake. The example is seriously weakened if it is presumed that Jesus wasn't God, and it would violate many scriptures that present the deity of Christ.

DISCIPLESHIP QUESTIONS

1. Was Jesus totally equal with God?

2. *Discussion question:* What are your thoughts on Jesus laying aside His divine rights and privileges in order to take the form of a servant and be made in the likeness of man?

3. What happens if it presumed that Jesus wasn't God?

But made himself of no reputation, and took upon him the form of a servant, and was made in the likeness of men:

PHILIPPIANS 2:7

LIFE FOR TODAY STUDY BIBLE NOTES:

- The decision for Jesus to become flesh was not forced upon Him. He chose that path of His own volition.

- The phrase **"made himself of no reputation"** is simply describing how Jesus humbled Himself. The *American Heritage Dictionary* defines *reputation* as "1. The general estimation in which a person is held by the public. 2. The state or situation of being held in high esteem." Jesus came from being recognized and worshiped by all the hosts of heaven as the Supreme God, to being a man, despised and rejected.

- The Creator became the creation. The Lord became the servant. The Highest became the lowest. All of this was done because of God's great love for us.

LIVING COMMENTARY NOTE:

Jesus was Almighty God. Yet, He laid aside His glory and became a man. He was a sinless man but a man nonetheless. What humility that the Creator would become His own creation. Notice that it says Jesus did all this to Himself. He didn't just consent to the Father and let the Father do this. This was His choice and actions.

The *New International Version* says that Jesus took on the very nature of a servant. The Greek word *morphe* that was translated **"form"** in the *King James Version* and **"nature"** in the *NIV* literally means "shape; figuratively, nature" (*Strong's Concordance*). This Greek word was only used three times in Scripture: Mark 16:12; Philippians 2:6, and this verse. In each of those three times, it was translated **"form."** This very context prohibits the translation **"nature,"** since it goes on to say **"in the likeness of men."**

Jesus took on the form, or likeness, of mankind. He had a sinless physical body, but it was still a physical body. In the spirit, however, He was Lord at

PHILIPPIANS 2:7 *(Continued)*

LIVING COMMENTARY NOTE:

His birth (Luke 2:11). He didn't have a sinful human nature.

DISCIPLESHIP QUESTIONS

1. *Discussion question:* What differences, if any, do you think it would make to Christianity if Jesus had been forced to come to earth instead of choosing to do so Himself?

2. How does this verse describe Jesus humbling Himself?

3. The _____ became the creation. The Lord became the _____. The _____ became the lowest.

And being found in fashion as a man, he humbled himself, and became obedient unto death, even the death of the cross.

PHILIPPIANS 2:8

LIFE FOR TODAY STUDY BIBLE NOTES:

• It is very significant that Jesus was **"found"** in fashion as a man. Jesus was the preexistent God who chose to become a man so that He could redeem us by His own blood sacrifice. When He became a man, He was still 100 percent God in His spirit, but His physical body was 100 percent human. His body was sinless, but it was still flesh and subject to the natural things everyone experiences. The physical Jesus had to grow in wisdom and in stature (Luke 2:52).

When Jesus was born, His physical mind did not know all things. He had to be taught how to talk, walk, eat, and so forth. He had to learn that He was God in the flesh and accept that by faith. That's why the word **"found"** is used in this verse. He found Himself in the form of a man. His physical mind grew in awareness of who He was. He had the witness in His spirit, but His physical mind had to "take it by faith"—the same way that we do when we believe who we are in the spiritual realm.

When Satan tempted Jesus in the wilderness, he began by saying, **"If thou be the Son of God"** (Matt. 4:3, 6; Luke 4:3, and 9). Satan was not just expressing his own doubts; he was trying to get Jesus to doubt who He was. Jesus' mental comprehension of His deity was something He learned and took by faith. Jesus had to become aware of His true identity through revelation knowledge.

• Remember that Paul was using Jesus as an example of how we should **"let nothing be done through strife or vainglory; but in lowliness of mind let each esteem other better than**

LIVING COMMENTARY NOTE:

Who found Jesus in the form of man? I believe this is speaking of Jesus finding Himself in the form of a man. Jesus existed as God before He came to this earth as a man. But when He took on human form, He took on the human form of a child. He didn't come out of the womb speaking Hebrew. He had to learn how to walk, talk, eat, and think. As the Scripture says in Luke 2:52, **"And Jesus increased in wisdom and stature, and in favour with God and man."** Jesus had to learn who He was!

Jesus' spirit was perfect and completely God, even as a child. The angels proclaimed Him Lord at His birth (Luke 2:11). But His physical mind was limited. It was sinless but limited nonetheless. It had to be taught, and there were times when He had to go beyond the limits of even His sinless mind and operate in the power of His eternal spirit (John 11:33 with Rom. 8:26). The Holy Spirit within Jesus certainly prompted Him and enlightened Him as to His true identity, but He had to educate His mind to that truth and accept it by faith. This is

PHILIPPIANS 2:8 (Continued)

LIFE FOR TODAY STUDY BIBLE NOTES:

themselves. Look not every man on his own things, but every man also on the things of others" (Phil. 2:3-4). Jesus is the supreme example of selflessness and putting others ahead of Himself.

We see clearly from Jesus' example that the way to exaltation in God's kingdom comes through humility and servanthood to others. Paul's example of Christ's humiliation is not only a lesson in Christology but also an example to all believers of what greatness in God's kingdom entails. Let this attitude of heart, Paul declared, taken from the example of Jesus Christ, continue to motivate all true believers in Jesus Christ.

LIVING COMMENTARY NOTE:

why Satan began each of his temptations to Christ with the words **"If thou be the Son of God"** (Matt. 4:1-11 and Luke 4:1-13). He was trying to get Jesus into insecurity about who He was, and to get Him to do something to prove it.

Likewise, we have to go against our limited physical senses and accept by faith our new identities in Christ.

DISCIPLESHIP QUESTIONS

1. How was Jesus born?

2. *Discussion question:* What benefits or hindrances do you think Jesus encountered as He grew in wisdom and in stature?

Wherefore God also hath highly exalted him, and given him a name which is above every name:

PHILIPPIANS 2:9

LIFE FOR TODAY STUDY BIBLE NOTES:

- The exaltation cited in this verse is in reference to Christ's ascension and glorification at the right hand of the Father. Because of Christ's humility and obedience, God has given Him a name that is above every name in heaven, in earth, and under the earth (Phil. 2:10). There is no exemption for anyone or anything from coming under the Lordship of Jesus. He is Lord of **all**.

- Jesus has not only been exalted above every being that has a name, but He is also highly exalted above anything else that can be named. If you can put a name on it, Jesus is above it. Sickness, poverty, depression, anger—everything has to bow its knee to the Lordship of Jesus.

LIVING COMMENTARY NOTE:

Jesus made sacrifices that no one else has ever made. He not only sacrificed His physical life for us, but He also left His eternal position as God to become a man. He gave up His position as God to become a God-man. Therefore, God the Father has rewarded Him by giving Him a name that is above all others.

DISCIPLESHIP QUESTIONS

1. What sort of name has Jesus been given?

2. What are some of the sacrifices that Jesus made?

3. *Discussion question:* What does the sentence "If you can put a name on it, Jesus is above it" mean to you?

4. *Discussion question:* In what ways could this affect your prayer life?

5. Sickness, poverty, depression, anger—everything has to bow its knee to the _____ of Jesus.

That at the name of Jesus every knee should bow, of things in heaven, and things in earth, and things under the earth;

PHILIPPIANS 2:10

LIFE FOR TODAY STUDY BIBLE NOTES:

• Every knee of man, angels, and demons will bow and confess that Jesus is Lord. Those who have denied His existence will bow in worship. Those who have spent their lives rebelling at His authority will finally bow in submission. Every being from all ages will ultimately bow and worship Jesus.

If we bow our knees to His Lordship now, we will enjoy wonderful lives here and an eternity in His blessings hereafter. Those who deny His rightful claim to the Lordship of their lives will suffer for it in this life as well as the next and will still have to bow their knees to His authority anyway. There is nothing to gain and everything to lose if people refuse to make Jesus their Lord.

• The *King James Version* has inserted the word **"things"** three times in this verse. This word is in italics, indicating that it was not included in the original Greek text. Most likely, the word **"things"** refers to the angels in heaven, mankind on earth, and demons, or residents of the underworld. The *Today's English Version* translated Philippians 2:10-11 as **"And so, in honor of the name of Jesus all beings in heaven, on earth, and in the world below will fall on their knees, and all will openly proclaim that Jesus Christ is Lord, to the glory of God the Father."**

LIVING COMMENTARY NOTE:

The things in heaven that are being spoken of here are godly angels and the godly dead. The things on earth are living people. And the things under the earth are demons and those who have been committed to hell.

PHILIPPIANS 2:10 *(Continued)*

DISCIPLESHIP QUESTIONS

1. What are the things in heaven?

2. What are the things on earth?

3. What are the things under the earth?

4. *Discussion question:* Meditate on the *Today's English Version*'s translation of Philippians 2:10-11. What revelation did you receive?

And that every tongue should confess that Jesus Christ is Lord, to the glory of God the Father.

PHILIPPIANS 2:11

LIFE FOR TODAY STUDY BIBLE NOTES:

- Jesus Christ is referred to as **"Saviour"** twice in the book of Acts, while He is referred to as **"Lord"** over one hundred times. This emphasizes the importance the early church put on complete submission to the authority of Jesus in their lives. In the epistles as well, He is called **"Lord"** hundreds of times.

Romans 10:9 is probably one of the most important focal points of the confession of Jesus' Lordship. It states, **"That if thou shalt confess with thy mouth the Lord Jesus, and shalt believe in thine heart that God hath raised him from the dead, thou shalt be saved."** The *New English Bible, Revised Standard Version, Today's English Version, New International Version,* and *Williams New Testament* all translate Romans 10:9 as confessing **"Jesus is Lord."**

LIVING COMMENTARY NOTE:

This will happen. We either voluntarily confess Jesus as Lord in this life and receive all the benefits of salvation, or we will have to confess Jesus as Lord when we stand before Him and be committed to eternal damnation. But everyone will confess the Lordship of Christ.

DISCIPLESHIP QUESTIONS

1. What will happen if you don't voluntarily confess Jesus as Lord?

2. On what did the early church put emphasis?

3. *Discussion question:* Why is it important to view Jesus as both Lord and Savior?

4. Which scripture is probably one of the most important focal points of the confession of Jesus' Lordship?

Wherefore, my beloved, as ye have always obeyed, not as in my presence only, but now much more in my absence, work out your own salvation with fear and trembling.

PHILIPPIANS 2:12

LIFE FOR TODAY STUDY BIBLE NOTES:

- Here, the Philippians were encouraged by Paul to be faithful in his absence as they had been in his presence. Notice that he did not tell them to work **for** their salvation; rather, he told them to work **out** their salvation (see the next *Life for Today Study Bible* note at this verse).

- Salvation is what God did for us through Jesus Christ. It is the gift of God (Rom. 6:23) that can only be received by faith. When we put our faith in Jesus as our Lord, God puts salvation and all its blessings in us (Phil. 2:13), but we have to work it out.

The phrase **"work out"** was translated from the Greek verb *katergazomai*, and according to Wuest's *Word Studies from the Greek New Testament*, it means "'to carry out to the goal, to carry to its ultimate conclusion.' We say, 'The student worked out a problem in arithmetic.' That is, he carried the problem to its ultimate conclusion. This is the way it is used here. The Philippians are exhorted to carry their salvation to its ultimate conclusion, namely, Christlikeness."

Philippians 2:13 reveals there is a divine enablement that wills and is able to perform God's bidding in our lives, but there is an effort on our part too. We have to work it out. This work needs to be understood in the light of the labor spoken of in Hebrews 4. We are to cease from trust in ourselves and rest in the Lord. That takes effort.

- The *Amplified Bible* translated the last part of this verse as **"work out (cultivate, carry out to the goal, and fully complete) your own salvation**

LIVING COMMENTARY NOTE:

God works salvation in us (Phil. 2:13). That is to say that when we are born again, the Lord deposits in us everything He accomplished through His death and resurrection. We then have to work it out of our spirits and into the physical realm. It is a major step toward victory when we quit looking for our deliverance to come from the outside and start recognizing that it is already in us and we just need to get it out. We've already got it. It's not God's turn to move. He's already done His part. It's our turn to believe and appropriate what God has already provided by grace.

PHILIPPIANS 2:12 *(Continued)*

LIFE FOR TODAY
STUDY BIBLE NOTES:

with reverence and awe and trembling (self-distrust, with serious caution, tenderness of conscience, watchfulness against temptation, timidly shrinking from whatever might offend God and discredit the name of Christ)."

DISCIPLESHIP QUESTIONS

1. What do you have to do once you are born again and Jesus deposits in you everything He accomplished through His death and resurrection?

2. *Discussion question:* Why does deliverance come from the inside rather than the outside? List some of the scriptures you would use to verify this.

3. *Discussion question:* What steps have you taken to bring you to the realization that your deliverance is already in you and you just need to get it out?

4. *Discussion question:* This verse says to **"work out your own salvation."** How do you go about accomplishing this?

For it is God which worketh in you both to will and to do of his good pleasure.

PHILIPPIANS 2:13

LIFE FOR TODAY STUDY BIBLE NOTES:

• God is always leading our born-again spirits, under the influence of the Holy Spirit, in the direction of His will. That's what pleases Him. Yet, we have a say in what takes place in our lives. God puts it in, but we have to work it out (see my note at Phil. 2:12).

LIVING COMMENTARY NOTE:

The Lord not only gives us the ability to walk in total victory, but He also plants that desire in us. He makes us willing.

DISCIPLESHIP QUESTIONS

1. What pleases God?

2. Do you have a say in what takes place in your life?

Do all things without murmurings and disputings:

PHILIPPIANS 2:14

LIFE FOR TODAY STUDY BIBLE NOTES:

• When we let God work in our lives, to will and to do His good pleasure (Phil. 2:13), we become free from murmurings and disputings.

The word **"murmurings"** is the Greek word *gongysmos*, and it was translated in the New Testament twice as **"murmuring"** (John 7:12 and Acts 6:1), once as **"murmurings"** (this verse), and once as **"grudging"** (1 Pet. 4:9). Its Greek meaning carries the idea of "a murmuring, muttering" (*Vine's Expository Dictionary*) and a displeasure and complaining that is more private in nature than public; i.e., a "secret displeasure, not openly avowed" (*Thayer's Greek-English Lexicon*).

The word **"disputings"** was translated from the Greek word *dialogismos*. This word was also translated **"doubtful"** in Romans 14:1 and **"doubting"** in 1 Timothy 2:8. It carries the idea of arguing and quarreling that does not bring about the righteous life that God desires (James 1:20).

LIVING COMMENTARY NOTE:

Remember the illustration Paul was using? He was speaking of how Jesus made the awesome sacrifice of becoming a man and dying for our sins. How did He do it? He didn't do it with grumbling and complaining. He willingly submitted Himself to God's plan. Likewise, if we want to act like sons of God, we need not only to comply with His will but also to do it willingly. If we are willing AND obedient, we will eat the good of the land (Is. 1:19).

DISCIPLESHIP QUESTIONS

1. Did Jesus grumble and complain about submitting to God's plan?

2. *Discussion question*: How have murmurings and disputings affected your life, either through your own actions or the actions of others?

That ye may be blameless and harmless, the sons of God, without rebuke, in the midst of a crooked and perverse nation, among whom ye shine as lights in the world;

PHILIPPIANS 2:15

LIFE FOR TODAY STUDY BIBLE NOTES:

- There are two areas of our lives where we need to be blameless and harmless: in our spirits and in our flesh. Our spirits were made blameless and harmless at salvation, and this condition doesn't fluctuate according to our performance. Colossians 1:21-22 says, **"And you, that were sometime alienated and enemies in your mind by wicked works, yet now hath he reconciled In the body of his flesh through death, to present you holy and unblameable and unreproveable in his sight."**

The way we become blameless and harmless in our flesh is to cease from murmurings and disputings (Phil. 2:14). As long as we are murmuring or disputing (see my note at Phil. 2:14), we are not blameless and we certainly aren't harmless.

- The *New International Version* translated **"without rebuke"** as **"without fault."** The Greek word used here literally means "that cannot be censured, blameless" (*Thayer's Greek-English Lexicon*).

- Some of us are intimidated by the **"lights"** (witness) of other Christians. We feel our testimony is not as dramatic as others and, therefore, are fearful of witnessing. We need to remember how dark our world is. Instead of comparing our light to that of other believers, we should compare it to the darkness.

We live in the midst of a crooked and perverse generation that is so dark, flickering candlelight can be blinding. Any of us who feel that our light isn't bright enough just need to find a darker place

LIVING COMMENTARY NOTE:

Not every Christian shines forth the light God has placed in them. We only shine as lights when we do all things without murmuring and complaining (Phil. 2:14) and are blameless and harmless as the sons of God.

PHILIPPIANS 2:15 *(Continued)*

LIFE FOR TODAY
STUDY BIBLE NOTES:

to take it, and our light will become a beacon. We are the only light some people will ever see. We need to let it shine!

DISCIPLESHIP QUESTIONS

1. How do you become blameless and harmless in your flesh?

2. Why are some Christians fearful of witnessing?

3. *Discussion question:* Why is it important to let your light shine? What are some of your experiences with other people shining their lights?

Holding forth the word of life; that I may rejoice in the day of Christ, that I have not run in vain, neither laboured in vain.

PHILIPPIANS 2:16

LIFE FOR TODAY STUDY BIBLE NOTES:

• It is not enough just to let our lights shine through our actions. That is an important part of it, but just being good without giving God the credit for our goodness is not enough. We have to speak God's Word too.

First Peter 1:23 says, **"Being born again…by the word of God."** Holy living doesn't result in people being born again; the Word of God does. Our actions and attitudes are important to open people up to the Word of God. It's like plowing the ground to receive the seed. But it's the seed that produces fruit, not the plow. Likewise, it's God's Word that saves people, not our actions.

Paul coupled righteous living (Phil. 2:14-15) and speaking God's Word (this verse) together in these verses.

• If the Philippians had let their light shine (Phil. 2:15) by speaking God's Word (this verse), then Paul will rejoice on the Day of Judgment when he sees that his fruit (the Philippians) remained (John 15:16). He will know that his efforts were not in vain.

On the other hand, if the Philippians didn't persevere until the end, Paul's labor could have been in vain (Gal. 4:11).

LIVING COMMENTARY NOTE:

Paul's rejoicing was not tied to personal achievement or comforts; it was all about others. If he helped other people receive the grace of God and they prospered, he was happy. True happiness cannot be found in self-fulfillment. It always has to be in serving others. It is more blessed to give than to receive (Acts 20:35).

DISCIPLESHIP QUESTIONS

1. What was Paul's rejoicing tied to?

2. *Discussion question:* What is your rejoicing tied to?

3. Can true happiness be found in self-fulfillment?

4. _____ _____ doesn't result in people being born again; the Word of God does.

Yea, and if I be offered upon the sacrifice and service of your faith, I joy, and rejoice with you all.

PHILIPPIANS 2:17

LIFE FOR TODAY STUDY BIBLE NOTES:

- The Greek word used here for **"offered"** is *spendo*, and it means "to pour out as a drink-offering" (*Thayer's Greek-English Lexicon*). The figurative meaning of this word is "one whose blood is poured out in a violent death for the cause of God" (*Thayer's Greek-English Lexicon*).

Paul was thinking of his possible martyrdom. Shortly before his death, Paul wrote a letter to Timothy in which he stated, **"For I am now ready to be offered, and the time of my departure is at hand"** (2 Tim. 4:6). The word **"offered"** used in that verse was also *spendo*. These are the only two passages in the New Testament containing this word.

The sacrificial drink offerings of the Jews were usually poured out around the altar. The drink offerings offered in heathen sacrifices were usually poured upon the sacrifice. Paul was using a metaphor that was more understandable to the Philippian believers, who had been converted from paganism.

- Paul was saying that if he was martyred because of his efforts to preach the Gospel, he would have joy and rejoice. What an attitude! This reiterates what he said earlier in this letter about only wanting God to be glorified. It didn't matter if he lived or died as long as Christ was exalted (see my note at Phil. 1:20).

LIVING COMMENTARY NOTE:

Paul was speaking of losing his life. He was in prison for preaching the Gospel, and it was possible that they could condemn him to death. He was saying that if he was put to death for his stance for the Gospel, he would rejoice with the Philippians for the privilege of dying for the Lord. These first-century Christians considered it an honor to suffer for Christ's sake (Acts 5:41 and Phil. 3:10). They loved Jesus more than life.

DISCIPLESHIP QUESTIONS

1. What was Paul talking about in this verse?

2. *Discussion question:* Why do you think persecutors pursue martyring believers if it isn't an effective way of stopping the spread of the Gospel?

For the same cause also do ye joy, and rejoice with me.

PHILIPPIANS 2:18

LIFE FOR TODAY STUDY BIBLE NOTES:

• It is amazing that Paul would joy and rejoice even if he was martyred, but he was saying that the Philippians should joy and rejoice with him if that happened. It's an honor to be martyred. There are great rewards and a better resurrection to be gained for martyrs of the faith (Heb. 11:35). This is not the attitude of most saints, but it was the attitude of the Apostle Paul. It will also be the attitude of all of those who share Paul's belief that **"to die is gain"** (Phil. 1:21).

LIVING COMMENTARY NOTE:

In the previous verse, Paul said he would rejoice if the Romans killed him for his faith in Christ. Here, he was saying that the Philippians should likewise rejoice if the Romans killed him. To a true Christian, this life is not the focus. Believers are headed to a better life after they exit these bodies. If Christians really believe that, then the death of a fellow Christian should be a joyous occasion.

DISCIPLESHIP QUESTIONS

1. Was Paul telling the Philippians to rejoice if the Romans killed him?

2. Why?

But I trust in the Lord Jesus to send Timotheus shortly unto you, that I also may be of good comfort, when I know your state.

PHILIPPIANS 2:19

LIFE FOR TODAY STUDY BIBLE NOTES:

• We can learn a good example from Paul here. Not only did Paul lead the Philippians to saving faith in Christ, but also his genuine interest in their spiritual welfare led him to send his most trusted companion—Timothy—to them. If ever Paul needed Timothy at his side, it was then, during his imprisonment. Even in the worst trial of Paul's life, he was putting the needs of others ahead of his own.

Paul was willing to send Timothy to minister to the Philippians in his place. Paul's letter and Timothy's ministry would certainly have encouraged the Philippian church, and Paul was looking forward to the good news that he would hear from them.

LIVING COMMENTARY NOTE:

This verse, as well as Philippians 1:1, reveals that Timothy was with Paul at that time, during Paul's imprisonment in Rome.

DISCIPLESHIP QUESTIONS

1. What did Paul's willingness to send Timothy to the Philippians show?

2. *Discussion question:* If you had been one of the Philippians at the time of this letter, what do you think your reaction would be to Paul sending you his most trusted companion?

For I have no man likeminded, who will naturally care for your state.

PHILIPPIANS 2:20

LIFE FOR TODAY STUDY BIBLE NOTES:

- Paul had some wonderful companions who were mightily used of God, but there was only one who had the same way of thinking as Paul. Paul had just expressed one of his radical attitudes; he rejoiced even at the thought of death. We can suppose that Timothy had that attitude too.

Out of all the relationships we make in a lifetime, there are only a few that are "Timothy" relationships. These are special and low-maintenance compared to others. They just happen "naturally" (actually supernaturally).

- Paul stated of Timothy, **"There is no one else here who sees things as I do"** (*New English Bible*). The Greek word for **"likeminded"** is *isopsuchos*, and it is derived from two Greek words: *isos*, meaning "similar" (*Strong's Concordance*), and *psuche*, the Greek word for **"soul"** in the New Testament. Thus *isopsuchos* means "equal [or similar] in soul" (*Thayer's Greek-English Lexicon*, brackets mine)—one who sees things the same. Timothy had similar interests and concerns as Paul.

LIVING COMMENTARY NOTE:

Paul had a lot of associates, but none of them were as dear or faithful to him as Timothy. Why was that? It was because Timothy naturally cared for the condition of those they ministered to. Others might have followed Paul's instructions, but Timothy had Paul's heart. It came naturally to him.

DISCIPLESHIP QUESTIONS

1. *Discussion question:* Do you think relationships like Paul and Timothy's are important today? Why or why not?

2. What makes "Timothy" relationships different from others?

For all seek their own, not the things which are Jesus Christ's.

PHILIPPIANS 2:21

LIFE FOR TODAY STUDY BIBLE NOTES:

• There may have been many things that made Timothy **"likeminded"** with Paul (Phil. 2:20), but the thing that Paul mentioned was that Timothy was not self-seeking. That was one of Paul's dominant traits and the main trait that made Timothy a faithful messenger whom Paul could totally trust.

LIVING COMMENTARY NOTE:

Why did Timothy just naturally seek the benefit of others? Paul said it was because he wasn't selfish. Selfishness greatly limits what God can do through us. God isn't selfish, and His will guides us to do things that may not always be to the carnal benefit of ourselves. Until we die to our selves, we will always be resistant to following the leading of the Lord. People who are all wrapped up in themselves make for very small packages.

DISCIPLESHIP QUESTIONS

1. Until you die to your self, how will you be?

2. People who are all wrapped up _____ _____ make for very _____ packages.

3. The fact that Timothy was not self-seeking made him what?

But ye know the proof of him, that, as a son with the father, he hath served with me in the gospel.

PHILIPPIANS 2:22

LIFE FOR TODAY STUDY BIBLE NOTES:

• Timothy had proven himself. Many people desire to have others trust them as Paul trusted Timothy, but few are willing to earn that trust. Some even get upset if that trust is not extended toward them, and they try to demand it. Faithful people, however, are so busy being faithful, they never demand anything. If trust isn't given, they just work harder. Trust is a gift.

LIVING COMMENTARY NOTE:

Paul wasn't just emotionally attached to Timothy. Timothy had proven his love for the Lord and for Paul through his actions. Paul's feelings toward Timothy were not based in grace but in Timothy's actions.

DISCIPLESHIP QUESTIONS

1. *Discussion question:* What are your thoughts on the statement "Faithful people, however, are so busy being faithful, they never demand anything"?

2. *Discussion question:* Why or why not do you agree with the statement "If trust isn't given, [faithful people] just work harder"?

Him therefore I hope to send presently, so soon as I shall see how it will go with me.

PHILIPPIANS 2:23

LIFE FOR TODAY STUDY BIBLE NOTES:

- Paul was speaking about his sentencing. He was in prison in Rome and awaiting the sentence handed down from Caesar. Before he sent Timothy back to Philippi, he wanted to know the verdict so that Timothy could inform his friends at Philippi.

LIVING COMMENTARY NOTE:

Paul didn't want Timothy to go to the Philippians until he had all the news about the outcome of Paul's trial. Likewise, our Father doesn't want to send us to proclaim His message until we have it correct. Many people are binding the devil's hindrances to their ministry when it may be that the Lord hasn't opened the doors, because they don't have the complete message yet.

DISCIPLESHIP QUESTIONS

1. *Discussion question:* Why is it important to have the complete message from the Lord instead of trying to bind the devil's hindrances to your ministry?

But I trust in the Lord that I also myself shall come shortly.

PHILIPPIANS 2:24

LIFE FOR TODAY STUDY BIBLE NOTES:

- There are different opinions on whether or not Paul ever got out of prison, but this verse reveals that Paul was expecting to be released from prison. See also Romans 15:24, 28; and Philemon 22.

LIVING COMMENTARY NOTE:

Paul was facing possible execution at the hands of the Romans. It was possible they could kill him, and he was waiting to hear his sentence before he sent Timothy to them. But this verse makes it clear that Paul firmly believed that the Lord would have him released.

DISCIPLESHIP QUESTIONS

1. *Discussion question:* According to Philippians 2:17, Paul rejoiced at the possibility of being martyred by the Romans. Here in this verse, he expressed firm belief that the Lord would have him released. How do you reconcile these two perspectives?

Yet I supposed it necessary to send to you Epaphroditus, my brother, and companion in labour, and fellowsoldier, but your messenger, and he that ministered to my wants.

PHILIPPIANS 2:25

LIFE FOR TODAY STUDY BIBLE NOTES:

• Paul had just stated that he planned on sending Timothy to the Philippians just as soon as he learned what his verdict was (Phil. 2:23). He was believing that he himself was going to be released and that he would come to them in person (Phil. 2:24). Despite all this, Paul thought it was necessary to send Epaphroditus to them immediately with the latest news.

• Epaphroditus' name means lovely. He is traditionally thought to have carried this letter to the Philippians (see the subscript at the end of Philippians [found in some Bibles]). He is only mentioned by name twice in the New Testament: here and in Philippians 4:18.

Epaphroditus was the Philippians' messenger (this verse) and bearer of things (probably finances) sent to the Apostle Paul from the Philippians (Phil. 4:18). He was also a brother, companion in labor, and fellow soldier with Paul in sharing the Good News of Jesus Christ. He personally ministered to Paul's needs.

Epaphroditus became sick, nigh unto death (Phil. 2:27), because of the service he was rendering to Paul (Phil. 2:30). News of his illness had gotten back to his friends in Philippi, and Epaphroditus longed for his Philippian friends to hear the good news that he had been healed. This provided Paul with an added incentive for sending Epaphroditus back to Philippi. He could not only share news with them about Paul's situation, but he could comfort the Philippians' hearts when they saw he was well.

LIVING COMMENTARY NOTE:

Paul said in Philippians 2:23 that he was waiting until his sentence was given to send Timothy to them. However, he felt compelled to send Epaphroditus to them right away. That's because Epaphroditus was from Philippi, and Paul knew the Philippians had heard Epaphroditus had been deathly sick (Phil. 2:27 and 30). Therefore, Paul used Epaphroditus to convey this letter and give the Philippians relief when they saw Epaphroditus was well. Epaphroditus was ministering to Paul, and Paul was no doubt better off with Epaphroditus there. But he preferred the Philippians above himself, just as he had instructed them to do in this very chapter.

LIFE FOR TODAY STUDY BIBLE NOTES:

Paul showed the affection he had for Epaphroditus when he said that if Epaphroditus had died, Paul would have had **"sorrow upon sorrow"** (Phil. 2:27). Epaphroditus must have been a very lovely Christian, as his name implies.

• What labor did Paul do? It is true that at times, Paul had supported himself and his companions through making tents (Acts 18:3 with Acts 20:34). But Paul was in prison and had been for years. He was not doing physical labor.

Paul was speaking of the work of the ministry as labor. In 1 Timothy 5:17, Paul spoke of elders laboring in the Word and in doctrine. It takes effort for people to minister to others and keep themselves in tune with the Lord so that they can be effective ministers. Those who are looking for an easy job should not consider the ministry.

• Part of Epaphroditus' ministry to Paul was financial. In Philippians 4:10, Paul said the Philippians' care for him had flourished again. Then in Philippians 4:15, Paul commended the Philippians for their financial contributions to his ministry. In Philippians 4:18, Paul spoke of receiving through Epaphroditus their financial aid once again.

DISCIPLESHIP QUESTIONS

1. *Discussion question:* How would you feel if, like Paul and Epaphroditus, a minister you were under sent you to minister to a group of people, even though that minister was in a time of need?

2. What was the twofold benefit in sending Epaphroditus to the Philippians?

3. What would have been Paul's reaction to Epaphroditus' death?

For he longed after you all, and was full of heaviness, because that ye had heard that he had been sick.

PHILIPPIANS 2:26

LIFE FOR TODAY STUDY BIBLE NOTES:

- Paul's statements about Epaphroditus give us clues as to how long Paul had been imprisoned in Rome at the time this letter was written.

The Philippians had to hear that Paul had finally reached Rome. In those days, news of Paul's whereabouts was not sent to them by means of telecommunications. An individual had to physically travel from Rome to Philippi and deliver the message. This would have taken a minimum of weeks and possibly a month or more. Then the Philippians had to send Epaphroditus with aid for Paul from Philippi to Rome, and that would again have entailed lengthy travel.

Once Epaphroditus reached Rome, a period of at least two months would have elapsed since Paul had reached Rome. It could easily have been longer. Then Epaphroditus became ill. News of his illness had to travel back to Philippi, and the Philippians' response had to travel back to Rome, for Epaphroditus to know that the Philippians had heard of his sickness.

The shortest time in which these events could have taken place would have been a minimum of three to four months, and it could easily have taken place over a year's time. Paul was imprisoned in Rome for two whole years (Acts 28:30). This letter was written at least months after Paul arrived in Rome and possibly toward the latter part of his Roman imprisonment (see *Date and Place of Writing* in the *Introduction to Philippians* at the beginning of this book).

LIVING COMMENTARY NOTE:

There was a powerful bond of love between Epaphroditus and the people in Philippi. It took weeks for news to travel by word of mouth between Rome and Philippi. Epaphroditus knew the Philippians who loved him would be very concerned about his condition. He was longing for them to be comforted.

PHILIPPIANS 2:26 *(Continued)*

DISCIPLESHIP QUESTIONS

1. *Discussion question:* What does it say about Epaphroditus and his relationship with the Philippians that he longed for them to be comforted?

2. What does this verse reveal about how long Paul had been imprisoned in Rome at the time this letter was written?

For indeed he was sick nigh unto death: but God had mercy on him; and not on him only, but on me also, lest I should have sorrow upon sorrow.

PHILIPPIANS 2:27

LIFE FOR TODAY STUDY BIBLE NOTES:

- Some people have interpreted Paul's statements here to say that healing is not a "right" for the people of God, but a gift that is sometimes given and sometimes withheld at God's discretion. That is not what Paul was saying. Healing has been purchased for believers as part of the atonement of Christ (Matt. 8:17). The Lord would no more refuse to heal believers than He would refuse to forgive them.

That does not mean that we deserve healing; we don't. It is a gift of God, just as salvation is a gift of God (Rom. 6:23 and Eph. 2:8). We don't deserve to have our sins forgiven. We cannot demand salvation from the Lord, but we can expect it. Likewise, healing has been purchased for us through the atonement of Christ. Healing belongs to us. But it is still the mercy of God that has provided healing, and every act of healing is an act of mercy.

- Paul's statement reveals that the Lord healed Epaphroditus not only for his sake but also for Paul's sake. This illustrates the power of intercession. We can make a difference in the way God deals with another individual. There are many examples of God showing mercy toward someone because of the intercession of another (Gen. 19:29, 2 Sam. 9:1, 1 Kin. 11:11-13, and 2 Kin. 8:19).

LIVING COMMENTARY NOTE:

Healing is a done deal. It was purchased for us by the atonement of Christ. But it's a love gift. None of us deserve it. Therefore, it is totally accurate to say it's the mercy of God that we get healed. This is not expressing the idea that some get healed and others don't, depending on how God feels at the moment.

PHILIPPIANS 2:27 *(Continued)*

DISCIPLESHIP QUESTIONS

1. Is it totally accurate to say that it's the mercy of God that you are healed?

2. Is this verse expressing the idea that some get healed and other don't, depending on how God feels at the moment?

3. You can't demand salvation (or healing) from the Lord, but you can _____ it.

4. *Discussion question:* How has healing being a part of the Atonement made a difference in your life and in your ministry to others?

I sent him therefore the more carefully, that, when ye see him again, ye may rejoice, and that I may be the less sorrowful.

PHILIPPIANS 2:28

LIFE FOR TODAY STUDY BIBLE NOTES:

- Paul was not living a life of depression. He had already stated that he was rejoicing through all his persecutions (Phil. 1:18 and 2:17-18). He continued in this letter to admonish the Philippians to live lives of joy (Phil. 3:1 and 4:4-8). Paul certainly lived what he preached.

Paul's joy was not in physical things; his joy was totally in the Lord (Phil. 1:21). In the natural, there were depressing things in his life, and there was, no doubt, the temptation to be sorrowful. Bad things do happen to good people, and we Christians are not exempt from problems and hardships. Sorrow comes into all of our lives. Sorrow exists, even for us as believers, but we don't have to let it dominate us.

Paul had emotions, including the feeling of sorrow, especially for others (Rom. 9:2). Paul rose above these natural things by thinking on the purer things of God. He lived a full life of joy but not because sorrow didn't exist. Rather it was because he cast his sorrow over on the Lord (1 Pet. 5:7), and kept his mind stayed on things above (Col. 3:1-2).

Therefore, it was not inconsistent with Paul's faith to speak of being less sorrowful. He was saying that this would just remove one more situation that he would have had to deal with. This would be one less thing to be sorrowful about. Regardless, Paul was walking in the joy of the Lord despite all his circumstances, and we can too.

LIVING COMMENTARY NOTE:

The Greek word that was translated **"more carefully"** here was *spoudaioteros*. It means "more speedily, i.e. sooner than otherwise" (*Strong's Concordance*). Paul was saying that he sent Epaphroditus sooner than he otherwise would have, because he thought it would bless the Philippians to see he had fully recovered from his sickness. If the Philippians were blessed, then Paul would be blessed.

Paul wasn't speaking of sorrow here as many people do today. He was simply saying that he would feel better knowing that the Philippians' concerns about Epaphroditus would be alleviated.

DISCIPLESHIP QUESTIONS

1. What does the phrase **"more carefully"** mean in this verse?

2. Sorrow exists, even for you as a believer, but what can you do?

Receive him therefore in the Lord with all gladness; and hold such in reputation:

PHILIPPIANS 2:29

LIVING COMMENTARY NOTE:

Paul was telling the Philippians to honor Epaphroditus. Some Christians think we aren't supposed to honor anyone but the Lord. It is true that we aren't supposed to honor anyone as much as the Lord, but the Lord said that those who honor Him, He would honor (1 Sam. 2:30). In this day—where we idolize movie stars, athletes, and many other people who are morally bankrupt—we need Christian heroes. Christian heroes are those who, like Epaphroditus, have put their own lives in jeopardy in order to follow God's will.

DISCIPLESHIP QUESTIONS

1. *Discussion question:* What are some ways you can express honor to Christian heroes?

Because for the work of Christ he was nigh unto death, not regarding his life, to supply your lack of service toward me.

PHILIPPIANS 2:30

LIFE FOR TODAY STUDY BIBLE NOTES:

• Paul stated that Epaphroditus' sickness was a direct result of the way he had neglected himself in his effort to serve Paul. Apparently, Epaphroditus had depleted his own strength in his service to Paul to the point that he succumbed to some type of sickness.

LIVING COMMENTARY NOTE:

Ephaproditus' sickness was linked to his service to the Lord and Paul. Paul didn't say what the problem was, but it could have been brought on by exhaustion.

DISCIPLESHIP QUESTIONS

1. *Discussion question:* Do you agree with the thought that Epaphroditus' sickness was brought on by exhaustion from his work in the ministry?

2. *Discussion question:* How would you handle a situation similar to Epaphroditus'?

PHILIPPIANS 2
Answer Key

PHILIPPIANS 2:1

1. Because what God offers is so much more in quantity and quality than anything the world has to offer

2. *Discussion question*

PHILIPPIANS 2:2

1. To walk in love with the brethren

2. Pride—it is the root of all division (Prov. 13:10)

3. *Discussion question*

PHILIPPIANS 2:3

1. **"Strife" / "esteem" / "themselves"**

2. Lowliness of mind, or considering others better than yourself

3. Jesus

4. *Discussion question*

5. *Discussion question*

PHILIPPIANS 2:4

1. No

2. *Discussion question*

3. *Discussion question*

PHILIPPIANS 2:5

1. He took the form of flesh so that He could know exactly how you feel, and He gave up everything so He could identify with you

2. *Discussion question*

PHILIPPIANS 2:6

1. Yes

2. *Discussion question*

3. This example is weakened, and it would violate many scriptures that present the deity of Christ

PHILIPPIANS 2:7

1. *Discussion question*

2. By saying that He **"made himself of no reputation"**

3. Creator / servant / Highest

PHILIPPIANS 2:8

1. He was born a man, His spirit was 100 percent God and His body was 100 percent human, and He had to grow in wisdom and in stature (Luke 2:52)

2. *Discussion question*

PHILIPPIANS 2:9

1. One that is above every name

2. He sacrificed His physical life, and He left His eternal position as God to become a man

3. *Discussion question*

4. *Discussion question*

5. Lordship

PHILIPPIANS 2:10

1. Godly angels and the godly dead

2. Living people

3. Demons and those who have been committed to hell

4. *Discussion question*

PHILIPPIANS 2:11

1. You will have to confess Him as Lord when you stand before Him and be committed to eternal damnation

2. Complete submission to the authority of Jesus in their lives

3. *Discussion question*

4. Romans 10:9

PHILIPPIANS 2:12

1. Work it out of your spirit and into the physical realm

2. *Discussion question*

3. *Discussion question*

4. *Discussion question*

PHILIPPIANS 2:13

1. Always leading your born-again spirit, under the influence of the Holy Spirit, in the direction of His will

2. Yes

PHILIPPIANS 2:14

1. No, He willingly submitted Himself

2. *Discussion question*

PHILIPPIANS 2:15

1. By ceasing from murmurings and disputings

2. Because they feel intimidated by other Christians and feel their testimony is not as dramatic as others

3. *Discussion question*

PHILIPPIANS 2:16

1. It was all about others, not his personal achievement or comforts
2. *Discussion question*
3. No, it always has to be in serving others
4. Holy living

PHILIPPIANS 2:17

1. His possible martyrdom
2. *Discussion question*

PHILIPPIANS 2:18

1. Yes
2. Because believers are headed to a better life after they exit these bodies, and if Christians really believe that, then the death of a fellow Christian should be a joyous occasion

PHILIPPIANS 2:19

1. That even during the worst trial in Paul's life, he was putting the needs of others ahead of his own
2. *Discussion question*

PHILIPPIANS 2:20

1. *Discussion question*
2. They are special and low-maintenance compared to others—they just happen "naturally" (actually supernaturally)

PHILIPPIANS 2:21

1. Always resistant to following the leading of the Lord
2. In themselves / small
3. A faithful messenger whom Paul could totally trust

PHILIPPIANS 2:22

1. *Discussion question*

2. *Discussion question*

PHILIPPIANS 2:23

1. Because it could be that God hadn't opened the door

PHILIPPIANS 2:24

1. *Discussion question*

PHILIPPIANS 2:25

1. *Discussion question*

2. He could share news with them about Paul's situation as well as comfort the Philippians' hearts when they saw he was well

3. He would have had **"sorrow upon sorrow"** (Phil. 2:27)

PHILIPPIANS 2:26

1. *Discussion question*

2. That he had been in prison a minimum of three to four months, and it could easily have been over a year

PHILIPPIANS 2:27

1. Yes

2. No

3. Expect

4. *Discussion question*

PHILIPPIANS 2:28

1. "More speedily"; i.e., Paul sent Epaphroditus sooner than he otherwise would have, because he thought it would bless the Philippians to see he had fully recovered from his sickness

2. You don't have to let it dominate you

PHILIPPIANS 2:29

1. *Discussion question*

PHILIPPIANS 2:30

1. *Discussion question*

2. *Discussion question*

PHILIPPIANS 3

Finally, my brethren, rejoice in the Lord. To write the same things to you, to me indeed is not grievous, but for you it is safe.

PHILIPPIANS 3:1

LIFE FOR TODAY STUDY BIBLE NOTES:

• **"Finally"** here is the Greek word *loipon*, and it literally means "the remaining, the rest" (*Thayer's Greek-English Lexicon*). It is a Greek expression that carries the idea of something left over (Wuest's *Word Studies from the Greek New Testament*). It is translated into English as **"besides," "it remaineth," "furthermore,"** and **"from henceforth."** This did not mean Paul was finished with the letter.

• The words **"joy"** and **"rejoice"** were used sixteen times in this short letter. This letter is one of Paul's most joyous epistles, even though it was written while he was in prison. The Bible clearly teaches that our joy is found in the person of Christ and not in circumstances.

The word *joy* is a noun, denoting a person, place, thing, idea, or quality. The word *rejoice* is a verb, describing the action of a person, place, or thing. When Paul told the Philippians to rejoice, he was telling them something that they were to do.

We can rejoice in the Lord always (Phil. 4:4), because rejoicing is an action, not a reaction to our environment. Joy is a gift from God that was given to us at salvation. It was placed within our born-again spirits (Gal. 5:22), and it doesn't fluctuate or diminish; it is constant. The Lord has put joy inside us, and now we are to "work it out" by choosing to obey this command of Scripture (see my notes at Phil. 3:12-13).

LIVING COMMENTARY NOTE:

Remember that Paul was writing this letter from prison. Yet, this epistle mentions rejoicing and joy more than any other writing we have of his. True joy is not dependent on circumstances. This is a command to rejoice. The word *rejoice* is a verb. That means it is something we do. *Joy* is a noun. A noun is something we have. We are to rejoice regardless of how we feel, because the truth is that in our born-again spirits, we always have joy (Gal. 5:22).

LIFE FOR TODAY STUDY BIBLE NOTES:

In the Greek, Paul's exhortation to **"rejoice in the Lord"** is in the present imperative. This essentially means that Paul was giving a command that is to have a long-term application—a command to keep on "rejoicing" as one's general habit and lifestyle.

- Notice that we are commanded to rejoice **"in the Lord."** Many people are not experiencing true joy, because their joy is in their circumstances; that is, they are waiting to rejoice when things in their lives are going well, and that doesn't happen very often. We are supposed to **"rejoice in the Lord."** That means we are supposed to rejoice in who the Lord is and what He has done for us. He never changes (Heb. 13:8), and His mercies and compassions are new every morning (Lam. 3:22-23).

- The phrase **"to write the same things to you"** refers to previous instruction given earlier to the Philippian believers. Paul was saying that repetition is part of the learning process. Peter spoke three times in his second epistle about the importance of remembering (see also 1 Cor. 15:2). Paul was bringing back to the Philippians' minds previous instruction for their own benefit.

DISCIPLESHIP QUESTIONS

1. What is true joy not dependent on?

2. *Discussion question:* You have joy in your born-again spirit, but you are to work that out through rejoicing. How can you develop and maintain a lifestyle of rejoicing?

3. What does rejoicing **"in the Lord"** mean?

4. _____ is part of the learning process.

Beware of dogs, beware of evil workers, beware of the concision.

PHILIPPIANS 3:2

LIFE FOR TODAY STUDY BIBLE NOTES:

• The New Testament uses the word **"dogs"** in both a natural and metaphorical sense. The Jews used this term when describing Gentiles, with the idea of them being ceremonially impure and sinful. In the Old Testament, the Lord used this term to refer to a male prostitute (Deut. 23:18, compare with *New International Version*).

• Circumcision was the dominant action and sign of the Old Covenant that God made with Abraham (Gen. 17:10-11). The legalistic Jews had lost the significance of the sign and were blindly observing the action, believing that circumcision itself produced salvation. Therefore, the issue of circumcision symbolized the difference between the Old Testament and the New Testament means of salvation (Acts 15:1).

Here, Paul used a play on the word *circumcision* by using the word **"concision,"** which means "mutilation" (*Strong's Concordance*). Circumcision, done the way the legalistic Jews did it (i.e., in order to obtain salvation), was nothing more than mutilation. It had no saving power whatsoever. In fact, it had a similar effect as castration. It stopped the regenerating power of the Holy Ghost in an individual's life. These Jews were mutilating men spiritually by adding legalistic rules to Christ's Gospel.

LIVING COMMENTARY NOTE:

I am not totally clear on whom Paul was speaking of when he said **"beware of dogs."** It is certain he was not speaking about the animals. Jesus referred to the Gentile woman as a dog (Matt. 15:26). Some commentaries say the Jews called all Gentiles dogs as a term of contempt. But Paul was the apostle of the Gentiles. He embraced Gentiles as having as much access to God through Christ as any Jew. Therefore, I would suspect this would be designating evil people, whether Jew or Gentile.

The word **"concision"** seems to be a slander against those who taught people had to be circumcised to be saved. In the Greek, it literally means a cutting or mutilation. Paul was saying that those who trust in circumcision were doing nothing more than mutilating their bodies. Circumcision without true faith in Christ was nothing more than mutilation. This would have been very offensive to those who embraced circumcision as essential for relationship with God.

PHILIPPIANS 3:2 *(Continued)*

DISCIPLESHIP QUESTIONS

1. What does **"dogs"** refer to in this verse?

2. *Discussion question:* How would you handle the legalistic ways of **"dogs"**?

For we are the circumcision, which worship God in the spirit, and rejoice in Christ Jesus, and have no confidence in the flesh.

PHILIPPIANS 3:3

LIFE FOR TODAY STUDY BIBLE NOTES:

• Who were the **"we"** Paul spoke of? He was not just speaking of the Jews who had been physically circumcised; Paul was saying that Christians are the true circumcised people of God.

In Romans 2:28-29, Paul revealed that true circumcision was a matter of the heart, not the flesh, and that true Judaism was through new birth, not physical birth. In Colossians 2:11, Paul said that spiritual circumcision was done by God without the hands of man.

The physical nation of Israel still has a very important part to play in God's plan. It figures prominently in end-time prophecy. But the physical nation of Israel has been displaced in importance by the spiritual seed of Abraham; that is, the church of Jesus Christ.

• The condition of a person's flesh is not the important thing. It doesn't matter if that flesh is circumcised or holy; it is the condition of the spirit that matters to God (2 Cor. 5:17). **"God is a Spirit: and they that worship him must worship him in spirit and in truth"** (John 4:24). **"Man looketh on the outward appearance, but the Lord looketh on the heart"** (1 Sam. 16:7b).

• In context, Paul was saying that those who put faith in their circumcision to save themselves are putting confidence in the flesh and not in God. Today the act of circumcision is not the issue, but acts of holiness are still deemed by many as essential for receiving salvation (Gal. 5:2 and 6). That is just as wrong as those in Paul's day who believed that being circumcised granted them salvation.

LIVING COMMENTARY NOTE:

Paul was speaking to Gentile Christians, and he called them the true circumcision. This is the same point he made in his letter to the Romans when he said, **"For he is not a Jew, which is one outwardly: neither is that circumcision, which is outward in the flesh: But he is a Jew, which is one inwardly; and circumcision is that of the heart, in the spirit, and not in the letter; whose praise is not of men, but of God"** (Rom. 2:28-29). Statements like these would have been very offensive to the Jewish legalists of Paul's day.

PHILIPPIANS 3:3 *(Continued)*

DISCIPLESHIP QUESTIONS

1. Paul was saying that _____ are the true circumcised people of God.

2. What did Paul say in Colossians 2:11?

3. *Discussion question:* Why do you think that some people today deem acts of holiness as essential for receiving salvation?

Though I might also have confidence in the flesh. If any other man thinketh that he hath whereof he might trust in the flesh, I more:

PHILIPPIANS 3:4

LIFE FOR TODAY STUDY BIBLE NOTES:

• Paul was saying that if anyone could trust in his or her own goodness, he would be the one. He was holier than all of them, yet as stated in Philippians 3:9, the righteousness that justifies people before a holy God must be a righteousness that is equal to God's. In order to receive this righteousness by faith in Jesus Christ, people must quit relying upon their own righteousness (which is of the Law, Phil. 3:9) and must trust in Christ **alone** for the righteousness that is of God by faith.

LIVING COMMENTARY NOTE:

Paul hadn't taken this doctrinal position because he didn't have any good works to trust in. He was holier in the flesh than any of his critics. In the next few verses, he listed all his self-righteousness. But he had learned that the only thing that makes people righteous in the sight of God is faith in what Christ has done.

DISCIPLESHIP QUESTIONS

1. What sort of righteousness is needed to justify people?

2. *Discussion question:* What are some areas in your life where you might still be relying on your own righteousness instead of trusting in Christ alone?

Circumcised the eighth day, of the stock of Israel, of the tribe of Benjamin, an Hebrew of the Hebrews; as touching the law, a Pharisee;

PHILIPPIANS 3:5

LIVING COMMENTARY NOTE:

Paul's critics were preaching that faith in Christ alone was not enough. They said people also have to be holy to be accepted with God. They boasted of their self-righteousness and condemned others who were not as holy. Paul was showing his critics that he lived a holier life than any of them. If they thought acts of holiness procured special favor from God, then Paul was holier than them all. Yet, he had found that all his holiness was not enough to grant him relationship with God. That only came through faith in what Christ has done.

DISCIPLESHIP QUESTIONS

1. *Discussion question:* Why do you think Paul's critics attacked him and his teaching when he had lived a holier life than any of them?

Concerning zeal, persecuting the church; touching the righteousness which is in the law, blameless.

PHILIPPIANS 3:6

LIFE FOR TODAY STUDY BIBLE NOTES:

• Paul's list of human attainments is impressive. He was a circumcised, full-blooded Jew of an outstanding tribe of Israel. As a Pharisee, he once guarded the Law with zeal. As for legalistic righteousness, he had been blameless. But in comparison to God's own righteousness, he had failed. The truth is that we all have sinned and come short of the glory of God (Rom. 3:23). It doesn't matter how good we are; we still need a Savior. Who wants to be the best sinner who ever went to hell?

LIVING COMMENTARY NOTE:

Paul was blameless, not sinless. **"All have sinned, and come short of the glory of God"** (Rom. 3:23). This means Paul was seeking to follow all the commands of the Law. He didn't achieve that standard, but no one could blame him for not trying.

DISCIPLESHIP QUESTIONS

1. Paul was _____, not _____.

2. What does Romans 3:23 say?

But what things were gain to me, those I counted loss for Christ.

PHILIPPIANS 3:7

LIFE FOR TODAY STUDY BIBLE NOTES:

• Before Paul met Christ, he was proud of his many attainments within the Jewish religion (Gal. 1:14). He was circumcised and had obeyed the Law of Moses. Concerning the outward observance of the Law, he was blameless (Phil. 3:6). His natural descent from Abraham gave him favor, so he thought. All that was necessary for his salvation, he had accomplished. He had done all the "dos" and avoided the "don'ts," but then he saw how wrong he was.

Natural circumcision was nothing. True circumcision is of the heart (see my note at Phil. 3:2). Natural descent means nothing—only the new creation (Gal. 6:15). Legalistic righteousness is to no avail and is as filthy rags (Is. 64:6). Paul gladly renounced his faith in himself and his own accomplishments so that he might receive Christ by faith along with all His accomplishments. *The Living Bible* renders this verse as **"But all these things that I once thought very worthwhile—now I've thrown them all away so that I can put my trust and hope in Christ alone."**

LIVING COMMENTARY NOTE:

Christ and self are like opposite ends of a seesaw. If one is up, the other has to be down. We cannot esteem ourselves and God at the same time.

DISCIPLESHIP QUESTIONS

1. What can you not do?

2. _____ _____ is to no avail and is as filthy rags (Is. 64:6).

3. *Discussion question:* Meditate on *The Living Bible*'s rendition of this verse (**"But all these things that I once thought very worthwhile—now I've thrown them all away so that I can put my trust and hope in Christ alone"**). What thoughts and revelations do you have on it?

Yea doubtless, and I count all things but loss for the excellency of the knowledge of Christ Jesus my Lord: for whom I have suffered the loss of all things, and do count them but dung, that I may win Christ,

PHILIPPIANS 3:8

LIFE FOR TODAY STUDY BIBLE NOTES:

- The phrase **"I count"** was translated from the Greek word *hegeomai*, and this Greek word means "to lead, i.e. command (with official authority); figuratively, to deem, i.e. consider" (*Strong's Concordance*). This means Paul didn't come to a place of failure where, through some sin or error on his part, he had become a "loser." He was the most promising student of Gamaliel (Acts 22:3). Paul chose to value his own effort as dung (see the *Life for Today* note on **"dung"** at this verse).

Many people come to the Lord in the midst of failure or personal tragedy. It is easy to see their own efforts as worthless in a situation like that. Those who are at the top of their game often fail to see their need for the Lord. They think they are doing quite well and therefore trust in themselves. That's why relatively few "successful" people come to the Lord.

The present-tense verb **"I count"** shows a habitual attitude and commitment to a long-term way of doing something. In other words, Paul continually counted as loss everything that would keep him from knowing Jesus Christ intimately.

Paul is an example to us all. He was the holiest—the best—yet he was nothing. If that was true of Paul, it is certainly true of us. Like Paul, we need to "count" **all** of our personal achievements as refuse so that we might totally rely on Christ.

- At one time, Paul had trusted the works of his own flesh as a means of acceptance with God. His faith had been in circumcision, ancestry, religion, zeal, and legalistic righteousness (Phil. 3:5-6). But

LIVING COMMENTARY NOTE:

Paul counted all his self-righteousness as dung in comparison to knowing Christ. What a word picture! All our self-righteousness is manure compared to knowing Christ. People frame their "manure" and hang it on their walls for all to see. Paul didn't boast in any of his accomplishments. His only claim to fame was faith in Christ.

PHILIPPIANS 3:8 (Continued)

LIFE FOR TODAY STUDY BIBLE NOTES:

here, he counted (see the previous *Life for Today* note at this verse) them all loss that he might gain Christ. In fact, Paul used the term **"dung"** (see the *Life for Today* note on **"dung"** at this verse) to describe how little he valued anything that would separate him from the surpassing value of knowing Jesus Christ as Lord.

• Wuest's *Word Studies from the Greek New Testament* states, "Not only did he (Paul) forfeit all this when he was saved, but his parents would have nothing to do with a son who had, in their estimation, dishonored them by becoming one of those hated, despised Christians. They had reared him in the lap of luxury, sent him to the Jewish school of theology in Jerusalem to sit at the feet of the great Gamaliel, and given him an excellent training in Greek culture at the University of Tarsus, a Greek school of learning. But they had now cast him off. He was still forfeiting all that he had held dear, but for what? He tells us, 'that I may win Christ'" (p. 91).

Only eternity will reveal just how much Paul gave up in the natural to follow Christ. One thing is certain—he gained much more than he ever gave up. That's true of us as well. The reproaches of Christ are infinitely greater in wealth than all the riches of the world or the acclaim of man (Heb. 11:26).

• The English word **"dung"** was translated from the Greek word *skubalon*, and this Greek word means "what is thrown to the dogs, i.e. refuse" (*Strong's Concordance*).

• The word **"win"** here was translated from the Greek word *kerdaino*, and this Greek word means "to gain" (*Strong's Concordance*). It was translated

PHILIPPIANS 3:8 *(Continued)*

LIFE FOR TODAY
STUDY BIBLE NOTES:

"gain" nine times (Matt. 16:26, Mark 8:36, Luke 9:25, 1 Cor. 9:19-22, and James 4:13) and **"gained"** five times (Matt. 18:15, 25:17, 20, 22; and Acts 27:21). This is the only time in the New Testament that this word was translated **"win."**

DISCIPLESHIP QUESTIONS

1. Paul didn't _____ in any of his _____—his only claim to fame was _____ in Christ.

2. What do those people at the top of their game fail to see and why?

3. *Discussion question:* Why or why not do you see a need, like Paul did, to continually count as loss everything that would keep you from knowing Jesus Christ intimately?

4. *Discussion question:* What sorts of things in your life should be counted as dung so that you may win Christ?

And be found in him, not having mine own righteousness, which is of the law, but that which is through the faith of Christ, the righteousness which is of God by faith:

PHILIPPIANS 3:9

LIFE FOR TODAY STUDY BIBLE NOTES:

• There are two types of righteousness: ours and God's (Rom. 10:3). Our righteousness is compliance with the requirements of the Law. God's righteousness only comes as a gift (Rom. 5:15) and is received by faith (Eph. 2:8). God's righteousness is perfect. Our righteousness is as filthy rags (Is. 64:6).

• One of the key Greek words of this passage is *dikaiosune*, which was translated **"righteousness."** It is hard for one English word to portray all that this means. A paraphrase of Paul's thinking may be "a right relationship or right standing before a holy God." Paul sought to establish his own righteousness—that is, a righteousness based on his own actions—in order to be pleasing unto God. He found that it was no more acceptable before God than the refuse thrown upon the garbage heap (see the *Life for Today* note on **"dung"** at Phil. 3:8).

Right standing before a holy God is not to be achieved in the keeping of the Law but in humble trust in the Person and work of Jesus Christ. Those who are trusting in their own righteousness cannot have the benefit of Christ's righteousness. The righteousness that gives mankind relationship with God is the **righteousness of God**, and it comes freely through faith in Jesus Christ (Rom. 3:22).

• Notice that Paul said he wanted the righteousness that comes through the faith **of** Christ, not faith **in** Christ. It is true that we obtained this righteousness by putting faith **in** what Christ had done for us. When we place our faith in Christ, the righteousness that Jesus

LIVING COMMENTARY NOTE:

This verse very clearly states that there are two types of righteousness. Our self-righteousness is dependent on how much our actions conform to the Law. That type of righteousness is necessary in our relationships with people but totally useless when it comes to relating to God. Then there is a faith-righteousness that comes as a gift to those of us who trust what Christ has done for us. That faith-righteousness is infinitely more in quality and quantity than our self-righteousness and is the only righteousness acceptable to God.

Notice that this faith-righteousness comes through the faith of Christ, not just faith in Christ. Yes, we put faith in Christ, but this is specifying a righteousness that was produced by the faith of Jesus. As we place our faith in Christ, the righteousness that He obtained through His faith and holiness is given unto us as a gift (Rom. 5:17).

PHILIPPIANS 3:9 *(Continued)*

LIFE FOR TODAY
STUDY BIBLE NOTES:

obtained by His faith becomes ours. We are possessors of Christ's righteousness, which His faith produced (Gal. 2:20).

DISCIPLESHIP QUESTIONS

1. What are the two types of righteousness?

2. Does faith-righteousness come through the faith of Christ?

3. *Discussion question:* Why do you think some people put their trust in self-righteousness instead of accepting God's righteousness provided through Jesus?

4. When you place your faith in Christ, what happens?

That I may know him, and the power of his resurrection, and the fellowship of his sufferings, being made conformable unto his death;

PHILIPPIANS 3:10

LIFE FOR TODAY STUDY BIBLE NOTES:

- Paul had given up everything that he might **"know"** Christ (Phil. 3:8). The Greek word used here for **"know"** is *ginosko*, and it was a Jewish idiom for the sexual union between a husband and wife (Gen. 4:1). It was not Paul's aim to know about Christ but to know Him and experience Him on the most intimate, personal level.

This involved knowing Jesus' resurrection power in the new birth (Rom. 6:4-5). It also involved sharing His sufferings. This does not mean the sufferings He experienced for our redemption but rather the sufferings brought on by one's allegiance to Christ. Furthermore, Paul's desire was conformity to Christ's death. While not denying that this may involve allegiance to Christ to the point of physical death, it appears that Paul meant the death to the flesh—life that is experienced through a vital faith union with Christ (Rom. 6:11 and 17-18).

- Paul said in Romans 12:2 that we are not to be conformed to this world but transformed through the renewing of our minds. Then he stated what we are supposed to be conformed to—we are to be conformed to the death of Christ. This is speaking of reckoning ourselves dead to sin and all its effects upon us in the same way that Christ is dead to sin and all its effects upon Him (Rom. 6:11).

LIVING COMMENTARY NOTE:

The Western ideal of knowledge is just mental. But the Eastern mindset saw knowing as experiential. Paul was saying he wanted to experience Christ and the power of His resurrection and the fellowship of His sufferings, being made conformable to His death.

Paul mentioned knowing Christ before he mentioned knowing the power of Christ's resurrection. Indeed, every aspect of the Christian life revolves around knowing Jesus in an intimate, experiential way. That has to be the main thing. Yet Paul didn't stop with just knowing Christ. He wanted to know the power that flowed from His resurrection too. We don't have to choose between the two. We should have personal relationship with the Lord that releases His supernatural power into our lives and the lives of those we meet.

Paul went beyond just knowing Christ and the power of His resurrection. Paul also wanted to know the fellowship of His sufferings. Paul didn't want suffering

PHILIPPIANS 3:10 *(Continued)*

LIVING COMMENTARY NOTE:

and neither should we. But it will come. Some suffering comes naturally, and then there is persecution that all godly people will suffer (2 Tim. 3:12). But everyone will suffer. That's the way it is in a fallen world. When it happens, God provides a supernatural comfort. It is this comfort, or fellowship with Jesus, that Paul was referring to. That comfort is so sweet that it makes the suffering seem like nothing in comparison (Rom. 8:18).

I like the *Amplified Bible*'s translation of this verse. It says, **"[For my determined purpose is] that I may know Him [that I may progressively become more deeply and intimately acquainted with Him, perceiving and recognizing and understanding the wonders of His Person more strongly and more clearly], and that I may in that same way come to know the power outflowing from His resurrection [which it exerts over believers], and that I may so share His sufferings as to be continually transformed [in spirit into His likeness even] to His death, [in the hope]."**

PHILIPPIANS 3:10 *(Continued)*

DISCIPLESHIP QUESTIONS

1. *Discussion question:* What does it mean to you to experience Christ and the power of His resurrection and the fellowship of His sufferings, being made conformable to His death?

2. Every aspect of the Christian life revolves around knowing Jesus in an _____, _____ way.

3. How are you supposed to reckon yourself?

If by any means I might attain unto the resurrection of the dead.

PHILIPPIANS 3:11

LIFE FOR TODAY STUDY BIBLE NOTES:

• Here, Paul was stating that he was looking forward to the resurrection that will bring him into complete conformity to the likeness of Jesus Christ. *Vincent's Word Studies* states that this expression, **"if by any means,"** was "not an expression of doubt" on Paul's part, but rather a statement "of humility" (Volume 3). Paul was not speaking of the general resurrection of both the just and the unjust; rather, he was emphasizing the resurrection of the believer out from among the dead.

• What did Paul mean? Was he saying that he hadn't received salvation yet? Was he insecure in his place in Christ to where he couldn't know until the resurrection day whether he would be accepted or not? Certainly not! That's the way some people view salvation, but that was not Paul's perspective.

The word **"attain"** was translated from the Greek word *katantao*, and this Greek word means "arrive at" (*Strong's Concordance*). Paul was saying that he had not yet arrived at the resurrection of the just, but that didn't mean he hadn't begun going in that direction. Salvation is the present-tense possession of all born-again believers, but there is a future-tense fulfillment that will be consummated at the resurrection of the just. As long as believers hold fast to their profession of faith (Heb. 10:23, see also 1 Cor. 15:2), their place in the resurrection is secure.

Note 25 at Philippians 3:11: The word **"resurrection"** here was translated from the Greek word *exanastasis*, which is only used here in this

LIVING COMMENTARY NOTE:

In Acts 24:15, Paul clearly believed that everyone would be resurrected from the dead—some to life and some to damnation. That general resurrection is not something we have to believe for. It will happen to everyone. Paul used a Greek word for **"resurrection"** that is used nowhere else in the Bible. It literally means an "out resurrection," or a rising from among the dead. This unique word is not speaking of the general resurrection but of the specific resurrection of the saints.

PHILIPPIANS 3:11 *(Continued)*

LIFE FOR TODAY STUDY BIBLE NOTES:

verse in the New Testament. It is very similar to the Greek word *anastasis*, and that word was translated **"resurrection"** thirty-nine times in the N.T. However, this word has the preposition *ek* added to it, which gives it the meaning of "out of" or "from" among the dead.

Paul was not speaking of the general resurrection in which even the unbelievers will participate. He was speaking of the "out resurrection" from the dead that only those who have saving faith in Christ will experience.

DISCIPLESHIP QUESTIONS

1. What resurrection is this verse speaking of?

2. *Discussion question:* What assurances does the Word give you that your place in the resurrection is secure?

Not as though I had already attained, either were already perfect: but I follow after, if that I may apprehend that for which also I am apprehended of Christ Jesus.

PHILIPPIANS 3:12

LIFE FOR TODAY STUDY BIBLE NOTES:

- Our salvation is a continuing experience. We don't just put our faith in Christ one time when we are born again (John 3:3) and then forget it. It has to be a continual trust and dependence on Jesus for our right relationship with the Father. Until we are resurrected with our glorified bodies, we have to hold fast the profession of our faith in Christ (Heb. 4:14 and 10:23). Paul was saying, "I haven't arrived, but I've left."

- The word **"perfect"** was used in Scripture to describe spiritual maturity as well as "being without defect or blemish" (*American Heritage Dictionary*). However, in this case, Paul certainly was spiritually mature, so that is not the meaning here. He was saying that he wasn't without defect yet. That wouldn't happen until the resurrection.

- Was Paul saying that his salvation wasn't secure and that he wasn't sure he would be among the saints? Definitely not! It is true that saving faith isn't just a one-time experience but rather a continual trust and reliance on Jesus for our right standing with God (see the first *Life for Today* note at this verse). There is a perseverance that is necessary in the Christian life. Paul was committed to Christ, and he expressed confidence on a number of occasions that he knew he would continue to walk in righteousness with God (Rom. 15:29).

Paul did not just want to attain to the resurrection of the just. Although he hadn't experienced that resurrection yet, it was purchased for him by our Lord Jesus, and Paul was in possession of that salvation. There are varying degrees of

LIVING COMMENTARY NOTE:

I haven't arrived, but praise God, I've left.

This isn't Paul expressing doubt about whether or not he would make the resurrection of the righteous. He was simply saying that this is so important that it was worth all his effort to ensure that he was among that number.

LIFE FOR TODAY STUDY BIBLE NOTES:

resurrection, however, even for the just. Paul was pursuing the highest resurrection, and that was not "in the bag."

Hebrews 11:35 says, **"Others were tortured, not accepting deliverance; that they might obtain a better resurrection."** This **"better resurrection"** apparently is referring to the varying rewards that will be given to believers. Martyrs will certainly be rewarded in a special way, making theirs a **"better resurrection."** All saints will be in the resurrection of the just, but some will have greater rewards than others.

In Philippians 3:13-14, Paul spoke of pursuing the **"prize of the high calling of God."** Paul wasn't trying to just finish the race—he was planning on winning first place. He wanted this better resurrection; that is, he wanted to bring more honor and glory to God than anyone else. He had not attained that yet, and he wouldn't know until the resurrection morning if he had made it. But that's the goal that the Lord had placed in his heart, and that was the one thing he pursued.

DISCIPLESHIP QUESTIONS

1. Is your salvation a one-time event?

2. What was Paul saying in this verse?

3. *Discussion question:* Think of some examples of any **"perfect"** (as used in this verse) believers you may know or know of. What can you learn from them?

4. *Discussion question:* What are your thoughts on Paul's example and pursuit of the highest resurrection?

Brethren, I count not myself to have apprehended: but this one thing I do, forgetting those things which are behind, and reaching forth unto those things which are before,

PHILIPPIANS 3:13

LIFE FOR TODAY STUDY BIBLE NOTES:

• By just about anyone's judgment, Paul was one of the most successful Christians who has ever lived. Here, he gave us one of his secrets of spiritual success: singleness of vision. Paul had one, and only one, goal in life. His heart was not divided.

The strength of the laser lies in the concentration of light onto one point. Likewise, singleness of purpose and vision is a necessity to victorious Christian living (Matt. 6:22). James said that if we try to master many things, we will fail (James 3:1). We have to set priorities and focus on those things. Paul had only one goal, which he described in these verses.

• Some people have misunderstood this verse and taught that we are to forget everything in the past. That is not what Paul was saying. The Scriptures teach us that memory can be a very powerful force for good in our lives (1 Cor. 15:2 and Eph. 2:11-13). In context, Paul was speaking about forgetting all the things that he used to trust in prior to his salvation experience (Phil. 3:4-8). Paul forgot his own attainments and focused only on what Christ had done for him.

Here, the word **"forgetting"** in the Greek is *epilanthanomai*, and it means "to forget...given over to oblivion" (*Thayer's Greek-English Lexicon*). The Greek verb for **"reaching forth unto"** is *epekteinomai*, and it means "'to stretch out to'...'to stretch' (oneself) 'forward to'" (*Thayer's Greek-English Lexicon*), as a runner that is running in the Greek games for the prize.

LIVING COMMENTARY NOTE:

One of the secrets to Paul's success was that he was single-minded. He only did one thing. He wasn't renowned for anything but his relationship with the Lord and what it produced. Our desire for worldly achievements dilutes what we can do for the Lord.

We can't reach forward until we get free from the past. Paul said he was forgetting the things that were behind and then reaching toward the mark of the high calling in Christ Jesus (this verse and Phil. 3:14).

PHILIPPIANS 3:13 *(Continued)*

DISCIPLESHIP QUESTIONS

1. *Discussion question:* How do you plan to deal with issues in your past that need to be forgotten?

2. What was one of Paul's secrets to spiritual success?

3. Does everything in your past need to be forgotten?

4. *Discussion question:* What are some things that you've experienced that you should remember?

I press toward the mark for the prize of the high calling of God in Christ Jesus.

PHILIPPIANS 3:14

LIFE FOR TODAY STUDY BIBLE NOTES:

• Paul used a metaphor of a runner running in a race. The Greek verb Paul used for **"I press"** is *dioko*, and it was used figuratively of one running swiftly in a race to reach the goal. It also carries the idea of one who pursues, seeks eagerly after, or earnestly endeavors to acquire the prize (Heb. 12:1-2). Since the **"prize"** of eternal life cannot be acquired by works of righteousness that we have done (Titus 3:5), Paul must have been thinking of the rewards that come from service to the Lord (see my note at Phil. 3:12).

LIVING COMMENTARY NOTE:

Paul wasn't just pressing toward any goal or mark. He was going for the prize. He wanted to do the very best he could and thereby win the race. Those who shoot at nothing hit it every time. Those who shoot at the stars may not always reach their goal, but they may at least hit the moon.

DISCIPLESHIP QUESTIONS

1. *Discussion question:* What are some of your goals in life, how do you think they line up with God's will, and how do you view them in light of the idea that "those who shoot at the stars may not always reach their goal, but they may at least hit the moon"?

2. Since the "prize" of eternal life cannot be acquired by works of righteousness that you have done (Titus 3:5), what must Paul have been thinking of?

Let us therefore, as many as be perfect, be thus minded: and if in any thing ye be otherwise minded, God shall reveal even this unto you.

PHILIPPIANS 3:15

LIFE FOR TODAY STUDY BIBLE NOTES:

• Paul had just said in Philippians 3:12 that he wasn't already perfect. Here, he spoke of those who are perfect and put himself in that number. The answer to this apparent paradox lies in the meaning of the word **"perfect."** As stated in my note at Philippians 3:12, **"perfect"** can mean spiritually mature, or it can mean "without defect or blemish" (*American Heritage Dictionary*). In Philippians 3:12, Paul used the word **"perfect"** to say that he wasn't flawless or without defect. In this verse, Paul was speaking of being spiritually mature, which he was. The *New King James Version* and the *New International Version* translate this verse by substituting the word **"mature"** for the *King James Version*'s **"perfect."** The *Amplified Bible* says **"spiritually mature and full-grown."**

• The "mind" that Paul admonished us to have was the single-mindedness he described in Philippians 3:13 (see my note at that verse).

• This is a great promise! One of the concerns many of us Christians have is "How can I know I'm thinking and acting properly?" This promise gives the answer. If we seek the Lord with pure hearts and singleness of purpose as Paul described in these verses, then the Lord has obligated Himself to show us anything that needs to change. In other words, all we have to do is keep focused on the Lord with pure hearts, and the Lord promised that He will show us any error. The only people who need to fear that they might be deceived are those who are not seeking the Lord with pure and single-minded hearts.

LIVING COMMENTARY NOTE:

The **"thus minded"** Paul was speaking of is the single-mindedness he had just described, where he was forgetting everything else and seeking only after God. When we do that, if we begin to think otherwise, the Lord will reveal that unto us. This is a promise that when we are putting first the kingdom of God, the Lord will show us if we begin to get off track. That's a wonderful promise. We don't have to be introspective. We just have to seek the Lord with all our hearts.

PHILIPPIANS 3:15 *(Continued)*

DISCIPLESHIP QUESTIONS

1. What does this verse promise you?

2. In Philippians 3:12, Paul said he wasn't already perfect, yet in this verse, he said he was. How do these verses reconcile?

Nevertheless, whereto we have already attained, let us walk by the same rule, let us mind the same thing.

PHILIPPIANS 3:16

LIFE FOR TODAY STUDY BIBLE NOTES:

• Paul had been stressing growth and winning, not just surviving. He wanted the Philippians to stretch themselves more for the glory of God. He didn't want them to stop what they had been doing. He wanted them to do more. In this verse, Paul reminded them to keep walking in the light that they had.

LIVING COMMENTARY NOTE:

These Philippians were strong believers, as Paul revealed in this letter to them. He was saying they should keep doing the things that got them to the place they were. This is the same point he made in Colossians 2:6, which says, **"As ye have therefore received Christ Jesus the Lord, so walk ye in him."**

DISCIPLESHIP QUESTIONS

1. *Discussion question:* What are some realistic goals to help you stretch yourself more for the glory of God?

Brethren, be followers together of me, and mark them which walk so as ye have us for an ensample.

PHILIPPIANS 3:17

LIFE FOR TODAY STUDY BIBLE NOTES:

- The Greek word that was translated **"mark"** in this verse is *skopeo*, and it literally means "to take aim at (spy)" (*Strong's Concordance*). Paul was telling the Philippians to separate themselves from the people who were not living according to the example Paul had set.

- Paul called upon the Philippians to imitate his own example and not that of the Judaizers or self-indulgent Christians (Phil. 3:18-19). An **"ensample"** is one who serves as a pattern, model, illustration, or sample.

Paul had suffered the loss of all things for Christ (Phil. 3:7), accounted all things dung in comparison to knowing Christ (Phil. 3:8), shared in the fellowship of Christ's sufferings (Phil. 3:10), forsaken his own righteousness and accepted Christ's alone (Phil. 3:9), forgotten those things that were behind and reached toward the prize that was heavenward in Christ Jesus (Phil. 3:13-14), and was walking according to the light and understanding of God's Word that he had (Phil. 3:15-16). Here, he was admonishing other Christians to follow that example (1 Cor. 11:1, 1 Tim. 4:12, and 1 Pet. 5:1-3).

LIVING COMMENTARY NOTE:

This is an amazing statement. It's not a proud or arrogant statement; it is the truth. Paul knew he was seeking God, and that resulted in blessing that would benefit those who followed his example. If we can't say this same thing, then we shouldn't be in ministry. If we can say this same thing, then we shouldn't let false humility hinder us from saying it.

Paul said a similar thing in Romans 16:17-19.

DISCIPLESHIP QUESTIONS

1. *Discussion question:* Why do you think some ministers stay in ministry even though they are not good examples to others?

2. *Discussion question:* Which of Paul's accomplishments in the Lord impacts you the most and why?

(For many walk, of whom I have told you often, and now tell you even weeping, that they are the enemies of the cross of Christ:)

PHILIPPIANS 3:18

LIFE FOR TODAY STUDY BIBLE NOTES:

- It is not clear to us who Paul was speaking of in these verses. Paul didn't give any explanation, because it was probably obvious to the Philippians to whom he was writing. They could have been professed Christians who were either legalistic or, on the other extreme, indulging in sinful pleasures. They are described as **"enemies of the cross,"** which implies "error" in doctrine or lifestyle. *Vine's Expository Dictionary* describes *error* as "a wandering, a forsaking of the right path…whether in doctrine, 2 Pet. 3:17; 1 John 4:6, or in morals, Rom. 1:27; 2 Pet. 2:18; Jude 1:11, though, in Scripture, doctrine and morals are never divided by any sharp line."

Further descriptions revealed their bellies as their god; this means they were led by their own fleshly desires and appetites. They gloried in that which they should have been ashamed of, and their hearts and minds were set on the things of this world. Paul wept as he declared their end being destruction. Paul often warned God's people of such deception (1 Cor. 6:9-10, Gal. 5:21, and Eph. 5:5-6).

- The people that Paul was speaking about were the **"enemies of the cross of Christ,"** yet he wept when he spoke of their destruction. That says a lot about the Apostle Paul. Paul was ruthless at times in defense of the Gospel, but his anger was not really against the people; rather, it was against the error they promoted and the damage it caused. Paul himself loved those who opposed him, even to the point that he said in Romans 9:3, **"I could wish that myself were accursed from Christ for my brethren, my kinsmen according to the flesh."**

LIVING COMMENTARY NOTE:

Paul derived no pleasure from seeing others fall while he succeeded. He wasn't self-seeking. He wanted the advancement of God's kingdom, not his own. His tears for those who were not truly serving the Lord were evidence of that.

What does **"enemies of the cross of Christ"** mean? It certainly doesn't mean being at war with the piece of wood that Jesus was crucified on. This is saying they were opposed to the concept that Jesus accomplished everything through His death on the cross.

These people may have even accepted that Jesus did die for man's sins, but they didn't accept that Jesus paid it all. They believed they had to add to what Jesus did for them by contributing their own holiness to the mix. But Jesus plus anything equals nothing (Jesus + anything = 0). Jesus plus nothing (except faith in what He did) equals everything (Jesus + 0 = EVERYTHING). See Romans 11:6.

PHILIPPIANS 3:18 *(Continued)*

LIVING COMMENTARY NOTE:

Anyone who preaches that Jesus' sacrifice was necessary but believers also have to be holy to obtain favor with God is the enemy of the cross. See Galatians 1:6-9.

DISCIPLESHIP QUESTIONS

1. Does being an enemy of the cross of Christ mean that you're at war with the piece of wood that Jesus was crucified on?

2. Jesus plus _____ equals nothing.

3. Jesus plus nothing equals _____.

4. *Discussion question:* Why will the enemies of the cross come to destruction? Find scriptures to support your reasoning.

Whose end is destruction, whose God is their belly, and whose glory is in their shame, who mind earthly things.)

PHILIPPIANS 3:19

LIFE FOR TODAY STUDY BIBLE NOTES:

• **"The cross"** (Phil. 3:18) is speaking of everything Jesus provided for us through His death and, specifically, the grace by which everything was provided (1 Cor. 1:18). Therefore, those who are enemies of the cross are trusting in themselves and their own goodness. They are their own savior, and they live to satisfy themselves, not God. So, saying their god is their bellies really is a very descriptive way of characterizing people who are enemies of the cross (Rom. 16:18).

• This last characterization of these enemies of the cross of Christ (Phil. 3:18) is amazing. He said they **"mind earthly things."** That sounds descriptive of most Christians! No doubt there are natural things that we all have to tend to, but there is a danger of being too earthly minded. As Romans 8:6 says, **"For to be carnally minded is death; but to be spiritually minded is life and peace."** We must put a priority on spiritual things and constantly be aware that a preoccupation with earthly things is not good.

• Notice that Philippians 3:18-19 is a parenthetical phrase. This means that Philippians 3:20 is a continuation of the thought Paul began expressing in Philippians 3:17. In Philippians 3:17, Paul told the Philippians to follow his example, and then in Philippians 3:20, he explained that his lifestyle was consistent with his heavenly citizenship. The parenthetical phrase contrasted the conduct of Paul's critics with his exemplary actions.

LIVING COMMENTARY NOTE:

These are very strong accusations against these people. Notice that along with all the terrible things he said about them, Paul ended this verse by saying that they minded earthly things. That was considered a terrible thing by Paul. Sadly, this is descriptive of most Christians today.

What did Paul mean when he said their **"glory is in their shame"**? Certainly, part of his meaning was that these people gloried in their accomplishments instead of only in what Christ did for them. Regardless of how people stack up compared to others, all have sinned and come way short of the glory of God (Rom. 3:23), which is Christ. Paul said, **"But God forbid that I should glory, save in the cross of our Lord Jesus Christ, by whom the world is crucified unto me, and I unto the world"** (Gal. 6:14).

Any boasting on our part shows we don't truly understand the work Jesus accomplished on the cross (Rom. 3:27). He TOTALLY saved us. He didn't just add to our good works

PHILIPPIANS 3:19 *(Continued)*

LIVING COMMENTARY NOTE:

and help save us. All our self-righteousness is as filthy rags (Is. 64:6). Therefore, those of us who glory in our goodness are glorying in our shame.

DISCIPLESHIP QUESTIONS

1. What does any boasting on your part show?

2. *Discussion question:* When you've gloried in your own goodness, what showed you that this was actually glorying in your shame?

3. *Discussion question:* What do you think it means for the enemies of the cross being their own savior?

For our conversation is in heaven; from whence also we look for the Saviour, the Lord Jesus Christ:

PHILIPPIANS 3:20

LIFE FOR TODAY STUDY BIBLE NOTES:

• This is the only time the Greek word *politeuma*, which was translated **"conversation"** here, appears in the New Testament. It was translated as **"citizenship," "homeland,"** and **"commonwealth"** in the *New International Version*, *Jerusalem Bible*, and *Revised Standard Version*, respectively. Paul used it to describe his citizenship as belonging to heaven.

• The Greek word for **"Saviour"** is *soter*, and it was used a total of twenty-four times in the New Testament.

Sometimes men, such as judges in the Old Testament, were referred to as **"saviours"**: **"And in the time of their trouble, when they cried unto thee, thou heardest them from heaven; and according to thy manifold mercies thou gavest them saviours, who saved them out of the hand of their enemies"** (Neh. 9:27, underline mine). Most often, God Himself was referred to as the Savior of Israel (1 Chr. 16:35; Ps. 24:5, 25:5, 27:1, 62:2, 65:5, 79:9, 95:1; Prov. 29:25; Is. 62:11; Mic. 7:7; and Hab. 3:18).

In the New Testament, the word **"Saviour"** is never used of just ordinary people. It refers to God the Father eight times (Luke 1:47; 1 Tim. 1:1, 2:3, 4:10; Titus 1:3, 2:10, 3:4; and Jude 25) and Jesus Christ sixteen times (Luke 2:11; John 4:42; Acts 5:31, 13:23; Eph. 5:23; this verse; 2 Tim. 1:10; Titus 1:4, 2:13, 3:6; 2 Pet. 1:1, 11, 2:20, 3:2, 18; and 1 John 4:14).

• The word **"Lord"** is a very significant word that appears in eight forms in the Old Testament

LIVING COMMENTARY NOTE:

The Greek word that was translated **"conversation"** here is *politeuma*, and this Greek word means "community, i.e. (abstractly) citizenship (figuratively)" (*Strong's Concordance*) Paul was strengthening his previous statement about minding earthly things. When we get this mindset that we are citizens of heaven and not this earth, it will radically influence our actions while here on earth.

PHILIPPIANS 3:20 (Continued)

LIFE FOR TODAY
STUDY BIBLE NOTES:

('adown, 'Adonay, gebiyr, Yahh, Yehovah, mare', rab, and shaliysh) and in four forms in the New Testament (despotes, kyrieuo, kyrios, and rhabboni).

Some of the predominant words in the O.T. are 'adown, used 335 times, and its corresponding noun 'Adonay, appearing 432 times. 'Adown means superior, master, or owner. When 'adown or 'Adonay refers to God, it is translated in the *King James Version* as **"Lord,"** with the first letter always capitalized.

The most predominant word translated **"LORD"** in the O.T. is *Yehovah*. It occurs 6,519 times and almost 50 times in its poetic form of *Yahh*. *Yehovah* carries the idea of God as being the existing One, who is always present. The *KJV* translates *Yehovah* in the O.T. as **"LORD,"** using all capital letters in our English Bible. The true pronunciation of this Hebrew word is not certain, because it was believed that God's name was too holy to pronounce.

The word most often translated **"Lord"** in the N.T. is *kyrios*, and it means one who is supreme in authority, the Master, Ruler, the one who has the right to control. It is sometimes translated **"Sir"** as a title of respect. The Greek Septuagint sometimes used *kyrios* for the divine name *Yahweh*. Some uses of the word **"Lord"** denote Christ's deity, as in John 20:28 when Thomas confessed Jesus as **"My Lord and my God"** (underline mine). One of the reasons for Jesus' death and resurrection was that He might be **"Lord"** of each individual who would personally trust in Him: **"For to this end Christ both died, and rose, and revived, that he might be Lord both of the dead and living"** (Rom. 14:9).

PHILIPPIANS 3:20 *(Continued)*

LIFE FOR TODAY STUDY BIBLE NOTES:

• The name **"Jesus"** is used 983 times in the New Testament, and it means "Jehovah is salvation" (*Vine's Expository Dictionary*). This name was chosen by God and implies God's saving work through His Son (Luke 1:30-31). He was named Jesus for He would **"save his people from their sins"** (Matt. 1:21). Jesus as Savior implies "a person who rescues another" (*American Heritage Dictionary*). It is very much like someone who rescues a person from drowning so that person might live. Jesus rescues people from perishing so that they might have eternal life and live with Him (John 17:3 and 14:3).

• The word **"Christ"** is used 571 times in the New Testament, and it means "the Messiah," the one "anointed" to rule (*Thayer's Greek-English Lexicon*) (John 1:41). God's Son, Jesus, is the Christ (Luke 23:2 and Matt. 16:16).

DISCIPLESHIP QUESTIONS

1. What will radically affect your actions while here on earth?

2. *Discussion question:* What does **"Saviour"** mean to you?

3. *Discussion question:* What does **"Lord"** mean to you, in regards to Jesus?

4. *Discussion question:* What does the name Jesus mean to you?

5. *Discussion question:* What does **"Christ"** mean to you?

Who shall change our vile body, that it may be fashioned like unto his glorious body, according to the working whereby he is able even to subdue all things unto himself.

PHILIPPIANS 3:21

LIFE FOR TODAY STUDY BIBLE NOTES:

• The human body is certainly one of God's greatest creations, yet Paul spoke of it as vile. This has to be understood in a comparative sense, and it speaks volumes about how wonderful our glorified bodies will be.

The Greek word translated **"vile"** is *tapeinosis*, and the *King James Version* translated it as **"low estate"** (Luke 1:48), **"humiliation"** (Acts 8:33), **"vile"** (this verse), and **"made low"** (James 1:10).

• The transformation from this physical state to having a glorified body will be a huge difference, but the power of God is easily able to accomplish it. If the Lord can work that miracle, surely the healing of our bodies or the freedom from other bondages is no problem to the Lord.

LIVING COMMENTARY NOTE:

Our bodies are actually wonderful creations. But compared to the glorified bodies that await us, these mortal bodies are vile. That is something wonderful to look forward to. It may be hard to understand how the Lord could take our bodies—which have been so defiled by sin—and make them glorious, but Paul stated that God's power is more than sufficient for the task.

DISCIPLESHIP QUESTIONS

1. *Discussion question:* Meditate on one of God's greatest creations—the human body—and compare it to the idea of a glorified body. What are some contrasts?

2. What is easily able to accomplish the transformation from this physical state to having a glorified body?

3. If the Lord can work the miracle of transforming this physical state to having a glorified body, surely the _____ of your body or the freedom from other _____ is _____ problem to the Lord.

PHILIPPIANS 3
Answer Key

PHILIPPIANS 3:1

1. Circumstances
2. *Discussion question*
3. You are supposed to rejoice in who the Lord is and what He has done for you
4. Repetition

PHILIPPIANS 3:2

1. Evil people, whether Jew or Gentile
2. *Discussion question*

PHILIPPIANS 3:3

1. Christians
2. That spiritual circumcision is done by God without the hands of man
3. *Discussion question*

PHILIPPIANS 3:4

1. A righteousness that is equal to God's
2. *Discussion question*

PHILIPPIANS 3:5

1. *Discussion question*

PHILIPPIANS 3:6

1. Blameless / sinless
2. **"All have sinned, and come short of the glory of God"**

PHILIPPIANS 3:7

1. Esteem yourself and God at the same time
2. Legalistic righteousness
3. *Discussion question*

PHILIPPIANS 3:8

1. Boast / accomplishments / faith
2. Their need for the Lord because they think they are doing quite well and therefore trust in themselves
3. *Discussion question*
4. *Discussion question*

PHILIPPIANS 3:9

1. Self-righteousness (ours) and faith-righteousness (God's)
2. Yes
3. *Discussion question*
4. The righteousness that Jesus obtained by His faith becomes yours

PHILIPPIANS 3:10

1. *Discussion question*
2. Intimate / experiential
3. Dead to sin and all its effects upon you in the same way that Christ is dead to sin and all its effects upon Him (Rom. 6:11)

PHILIPPIANS 3:11

1. A specific resurrection of the saints, not the general resurrection
2. *Discussion question*

PHILIPPIANS 3:12

1. No, it is a continual trust and dependence on Jesus for your right relationship with the Father
2. "I haven't arrived, but I've left"
3. *Discussion question*
4. *Discussion question*

PHILIPPIANS 3:13

1. *Discussion question*
2. Singleness of vision
3. No
4. *Discussion question*

PHILIPPIANS 3:14

1. *Discussion question*
2. The rewards that come from service to the Lord

PHILIPPIANS 3:15

1. That when you are putting first the kingdom of God, the Lord will show you if you begin to get off track
2. In Philippians 3:12, **"perfect"** means flawless or without defect—in this verse, it means spiritually mature

PHILIPPIANS 3:16

1. *Discussion question*

PHILIPPIANS 3:17

1. *Discussion question*
2. *Discussion question*

PHILIPPIANS 3:18

1. No, it's being opposed to the concept that Jesus accomplished everything through His death on the cross
2. Anything
3. Everything
4. *Discussion question*

PHILIPPIANS 3:19

1. That you don't truly understand the work Jesus accomplished on the cross (Rom. 3:27)
2. *Discussion question*
3. *Discussion question*

PHILIPPIANS 3:20

1. Getting the mindset that you are a citizen of heaven and not this earth
2. *Discussion question*
3. *Discussion question*
4. *Discussion question*
5. *Discussion question*

PHILIPPIANS 3:21

1. *Discussion question*
2. The power of God
3. Healing / bondages / no

PHILIPPIANS 4

Therefore, my brethren dearly beloved and longed for, my joy and crown, so stand fast in the Lord, my dearly beloved.

PHILIPPIANS 4:1

LIFE FOR TODAY STUDY BIBLE NOTES:

- The word **"therefore"** is tying what Paul was saying here to what he had said previously. Paul had just spoken of the Lord giving us glorified bodies. Because of this wonderful reward to the faithful, we should **"therefore"** stand fast in the Lord. All that we have to gain in the "sweet by-and-by" should provide us with plenty of motivation to stand fast in the "rough here-and-now."

- Paul addressed the Philippians twice in this verse as **"dearly beloved."** In this same verse, he also called them **"my joy and crown."** These terms expressed Paul's love for these saints and showed that they were very special to him.

This also revealed what Paul valued most. He wasn't after the recognition of mankind or their awards. What gave Paul joy was to see others experience the abundant life that only God can give. All the lives that had been changed by the power of God were like a crown that he wore proudly.

One reason Paul had the impact that he did was because he didn't see things as other people did. Others sought for earthly titles; Paul was after just one thing (Phil. 3:13-14).

- **"Stand fast"** was translated from one Greek word, *steko*, which describes a military soldier who stands fast in the midst of a battle. It is only the strength and power of the Lord that are able to make us stand and to keep us from falling (Jude 24). That is why Paul told the Philippians to **"stand fast in the Lord."**

LIVING COMMENTARY NOTE:

Paul really had special feelings for these Philippian Christians. In the first chapter, he said he rejoiced every time he thought of them, which was often. Certainly, one of the things that made them so close was their partnership with him in the Gospel, as he expounded upon in this chapter.

PHILIPPIANS 4:1 *(Continued)*

LIFE FOR TODAY
STUDY BIBLE NOTES:

Although this power is always available in Christians' lives, it will not work automatically. It must be personally appropriated by faith. Day by day, moment by moment, Christians must trust the power of the Lord—rather than their own power—for the victory over sin, the flesh, and the devil.

DISCIPLESHIP QUESTIONS

1. What gave Paul joy?

2. Only the strength and power of the Lord are able to what?

3. *Discussion question:* In what ways do you daily trust the power of the Lord, and in what areas, if any, could you rely on Him more?

I beseech Euodias, and beseech Syntyche, that they be of the same mind in the Lord.

PHILIPPIANS 4:2

LIFE FOR TODAY STUDY BIBLE NOTES:

• Euodias and Syntyche were women in the Philippian church who Paul said had labored with him in the Gospel (Phil. 4:3). This is the only time they are mentioned by name in Scripture. Euodias means "fragrance" (*Thayer's Greek-English Lexicon*), and Syntyche means "with fate" (*Smith's Bible Dictionary*). From this context, we can see that there had been a disagreement between them, and Paul was beseeching them to reconcile.

It is noticeable that Paul told them to **"be of the same mind in the Lord"** (see also 1 Cor. 1:10). The only way we can ever come into true unity is to find our common ground in the Lord and fellowship in those areas. There will never be, nor was there ever intended to be, unity in every area of our lives. We have different customs, personalities, and so forth. Our unity has to be **"in the Lord."**

The more our lives center on the Lord, the more unity we will have with others who center on the Lord. For those of us who hold our own lives dear and have not found the joy that Paul expressed when he said **"For to me to live is Christ, and to die is gain"** (Phil. 1:21), we will walk in very little unity. Our unity has to be **"in the Lord."**

LIVING COMMENTARY NOTE:

Most commentaries believe these were two women that Paul was beseeching to lay aside their differences. It is true that differences arise, as can be seen in this instance, but notice that Paul didn't accept it as an inevitable thing. He was calling for unity. Division is terribly damaging to the work of the Lord, and variances should be reconciled if at all possible.

PHILIPPIANS 4:2 *(Continued)*

DISCIPLESHIP QUESTIONS

1. It is true that _____ arise, as can be seen in this instance, but notice that Paul didn't accept it as an _____ thing.

2. *Discussion question:* What are some of the divisions and their subsequent effects that you have seen in your life?

3. What is the only way you can ever come into true unity with others?

4. Will there ever be, or was there ever intended to be, unity in every area of your life?

And I intreat thee also, true yokefellow, help those women which laboured with me in the gospel, with Clement also, and with other my fellowlabourers, whose names are in the book of life.

PHILIPPIANS 4:3

LIFE FOR TODAY STUDY BIBLE NOTES:

- The word **"yokefellow"** paints a picture of someone pulling together with Paul in the work of the Gospel, like yoked oxen. The strength of the oxen is increased by virtue of their being yoked together. The *Today's English Version* translated this word as **"faithful partner."** It is not clear whether Paul was speaking of an individual here or if he was referring to the Philippian believers as a whole. It is also unclear whether he was requesting them to help Euodias and Syntyche reconcile their differences, or if he was speaking of other help.

- Euodias, Syntyche, and Clement were obviously fellow workers who had labored with Paul in the Gospel. The Greek word for **"laboured"** in this verse is *sunathleo*, and it was used two times in the New Testament (Phil. 1:27 and this verse). *Sunathleo* was translated as "strive together for" and "labour with" (*Strong's Concordance*). "It is a word normally used of fighting a war or of a contest in an athletic arena" (*A Translator's Handbook on Philippians*, p. 126). It is also translated as **"worked side by side"** (*The Living Bible*), **"worked hard with me"** (*Today's English Version*), **"a help to me when I was fighting"** (*Jerusalem Bible*), and **"who shared my struggles"** (*New English Bible*).

- This is the only mention of Clement in Scripture. His name means "mild, merciful" (*Smith's Bible Dictionary*). Some people think this is the same Clement who became the bishop of Rome around the end of the first century.

LIVING COMMENTARY NOTE:

It is not known if the women Paul was speaking of here are the Euodias and Syntyche spoken of in the previous verse. Whoever they were, these women labored with Paul in the Gospel. It's unclear what that meant.

PHILIPPIANS 4:3 *(Continued)*

LIFE FOR TODAY
STUDY BIBLE NOTES:

• This is the only mention of the **"book of life"** by that name in Scripture outside of Revelation. It is probable that the book spoken of in Daniel 12:1 is referring to this Book of Life. Jesus told us to rejoice because our names are written in heaven, implying the Book of Life. The Book of Life is referred to seven times in Revelation (Rev. 3:5; 13:8; 17:8; 20:12, 15; 21:27; and 22:19), for a total of eight definite times in Scripture.

We cannot enter God's presence without our names being written in the Lamb's Book of Life (Rev. 21:27). Anyone whose name is not written in the Book of Life will spend eternity in the lake of fire (Rev. 20:15). It is possible to have our names blotted out of the Book of Life (Rev. 3:5). There will be books that contain records of our deeds by which we will be judged. Apparently, having our names written in the Book of Life will supersede anything else written about us (Rev. 20:12).

DISCIPLESHIP QUESTIONS

1. *Discussion question:* Why is it important to be a **"yokefellow"** to someone else in the ministry?

2. What is the importance of the Book of Life?

3. Will having your name in the Book of Life supersede anything else written about you?

Rejoice in the Lord alway: and again I say, Rejoice.

PHILIPPIANS 4:4

LIFE FOR TODAY STUDY BIBLE NOTES:

• Joy is something we have; rejoicing is something we do (see my note at Phil. 3:1). The reason most people don't rejoice always, as instructed here, is because they don't know that they already have joy (Gal. 5:22).

• Notice that Paul instructed us to **"rejoice in the Lord"** (underline mine). Our joy is in the Lord. That means that our joy is in our born-again spirits. Joy doesn't come from the outside in response to circumstances; it comes from the inside and is a fruit of the Spirit (Gal. 5:22). We always have joy, but we must choose to rejoice.

• Everyone wants to rejoice, and most people do rejoice at times; but Paul commanded us to rejoice in the Lord **always**. That seems unreasonable and impossible to most people. They think, *You can't always be rejoicing even through bad times!* But the Lord would be unjust to command us to do something that is unobtainable. Rejoicing at all times is not only possible—it is preferable!

It's true that we can't rejoice at all times if we are waiting for our circumstances to be good. Even in the few times when everything seems to be just right, we will have some sorrow because of past tragedies or future fears. Our rejoicing has to be in the Lord (see the first *Life for Today* note at this verse).

• This command (see the previous *Life for Today* note at this verse) differs from the thinking of most people to such an extent that they would think they were surely misunderstanding Paul. So, to leave no doubt that he meant just what he said,

LIVING COMMENTARY NOTE:

This isn't instructing us to be happy. Paul commanded us to rejoice. Rejoice is a verb—it's something we do—whereas happiness is a state of being. We may not always be happy, but we can always rejoice. We can rejoice regardless of what's happening to us, or Paul wouldn't have commanded us to do it.

This sounds so far removed from the way most people think and act that it would lead some to think that surely Paul couldn't have meant what it sounded like he meant. Therefore, he repeated himself just so no one would think he made a mistake.

LIFE FOR TODAY STUDY BIBLE NOTES:

he repeated himself. This emphasizes this truth and leaves no room for explaining this away—we are to rejoice in the Lord **always**.

• This is not a suggestion or a request from Paul. It is a command from their apostle, and it was inspired by the Holy Spirit. It is a command for us too. Those who don't follow this command are breaking the Word of God just as much as those who don't follow some of the moral laws, such as not stealing, not committing adultery, and so forth. This is a law of the Lord.

That removes any doubt we may have about not having authority over our emotions. If emotions were only uncontrollable chemical reactions to circumstances, then the Lord would be unjust to give us an impossible command and then hold us accountable (Deut. 28:47-48). But God is not unjust, and we are commanded to rejoice **always**. Therefore, we can and should control our emotions.

• The word *rejoice* is used, in some form, a total of 192 times in Scripture. Many reasons and occasions to rejoice are recorded in the Scriptures. The following are just a few:

- We are to rejoice before the Lord our God (Lev. 23:40; Deut. 12:12, and 18).
- We are to rejoice in God's salvation (1 Sam. 2:1).
- We are to rejoice because we are those who seek the Lord (1 Chr. 16:10).
- We are to rejoice in goodness (2 Chr. 6:41).
- We are to rejoice in God's mercy (Ps. 31:7).
- We are to rejoice when we sing to God (Ps. 71:23).
- We are to rejoice because our names are written in heaven (Luke 10:20).
- We are to rejoice in the light (John 5:35).

LIFE FOR TODAY STUDY BIBLE NOTES:

- We are to rejoice in hope of the glory of God (Rom. 5:2).
- We are to rejoice in the day of Christ (Phil. 2:16).
- We are to rejoice in Christ Jesus Himself (Phil. 3:3).
- We are to rejoice in sufferings (Col. 1:24).

Twice in this verse, Paul encouraged the Philippians to rejoice. This is even more unusual when we realize that Paul was in prison at the time of this writing. Outward circumstances may sometimes be against us, but inward joy can always be ours because we are **"in the Lord"** (Rom. 16:11, 1 Cor. 1:30, and 2 Cor. 5:17). We may be content in all situations, for God's Word says, **"I will never leave thee, nor forsake thee"** (Heb. 13:5) and **"in thy presence is fulness of joy"** (Ps. 16:11). No matter what our circumstances, we can always be glad, and take great pleasure in and enjoy the Lord.

DISCIPLESHIP QUESTIONS

1. You may not always be _____, but you can always _____.

2. Where does joy come from?

3. What are some of the reasons and occasions the Bible tells you to rejoice?

4. *Discussion question:* Select one of these reasons/occasions. What is an example of how you have rejoiced?

Let your moderation be known unto all men. The Lord is at hand.

PHILIPPIANS 4:5

LIFE FOR TODAY STUDY BIBLE NOTES:

• The Greek word for **"moderation"** here is *epieikes*, and it was translated **"gentle"** three times, **"patient"** one time, and **"moderation"** one time in the *King James Version*. The *New International Version* translated *epieikes* as **"gentleness."** The *New American Standard* says, **"Let your forbearing spirit be known to all men."** The *Amplified Bible* says, **"Let all men know and perceive and recognize your unselfishness (your considerateness, your forbearing spirit)."**

This word "originally indicated a thoughtful, considerate and decent outlook. Rather than hotly demanding his or her rights, whatever the cost to others, a person with this trait seeks peace in a calm way.... [This word is] opposite of an angry harshness that grows out of personal pride and a dominating selfishness" (*Expository Dictionary of Bible Words*, pp. 303-304; brackets mine).

• Notice that our moderation (see the previous *Life for Today* note at this verse) is to be known unto all. In other words, we are to let our light shine all the time (Matt. 5:14-16). Those who are only holy at church are Pharisees. If we can't be godly toward our customers or bosses, then we are not fulfilling this command. Our light is not to be put under a bushel but on a candlestick where it can give light to all who are in the house (Matt. 5:15).

• Paul gave a reason for letting this godly trait of **"moderation"** (see the first *Life for Today* note at this verse) be displayed before mankind: It is because **"the Lord is at hand."** Jesus is coming soon, and that means we will soon be facing our Maker. All of mankind needs to be ready, and we

LIVING COMMENTARY NOTE:

"Moderation" here could be referring to a number of things. The *New International Version* translated this as **"gentleness."** It certainly is referring to restraint of passions or actions or both. And this behavior is supposed to be so dominant in our lives that it is visible to all.

PHILIPPIANS 4:5 *(Continued)*

LIFE FOR TODAY
STUDY BIBLE NOTES:

are God's witnesses to get them ready. Therefore, we need to be about our Father's business of leading people to the Light. The way we do this is to let our lights shine, or let our **"moderation be known unto all men."**

• Paul expressed his belief on other occasions that the second coming of the Lord was imminent. In 1 Corinthians 7:29-31, Paul told husbands the time was so short that they needed to act like they weren't married. James made similar statements (James 5:8-9), and so did the Apostle Peter (1 Pet. 4:7). If this was their perspective nearly 2,000 years ago, how much more should we expect the coming of the Lord to be near. One thing is for sure—whether Christ comes in our lifetime or not, this is **our** last generation to work for the Lord. We need to take it seriously. This is not a rehearsal.

DISCIPLESHIP QUESTIONS

1. *Discussion question:* Why do you think a lifestyle of moderation is important?

2. Why do you need to let this godly trait of **"moderation"** be displayed before mankind?

Be careful for nothing; but in every thing by prayer and supplication with thanksgiving let your requests be made known unto God.

PHILIPPIANS 4:6

LIFE FOR TODAY STUDY BIBLE NOTES:

- Today we think of **"careful"** as meaning to be cautious, but 400 years ago, when the *King James Version* was translated, it meant to be full of cares or anxiety. Paul was admonishing these Philippian believers, who had been worried about his imprisonment (Phil. 1:12) and Epaphroditus being sick (Phil. 2:25-26), to cast all their cares upon the Lord. There is no better way to do this than to rejoice in the Lord all the time. Rejoicing makes us focus our attention on the Lord and His promises instead of on our negative circumstances.

- Most believers realize that anxiety and worry are not good and try to avoid them, but most believers do not believe that it is possible to live a life totally free of care (see the previous *Life for Today* note at this verse). Paul commanded us to be careful for nothing. That means there is nothing that we should be worried about. There are no limits to the peace of God.

- The way we keep from being careful (see the first *Life for Today* note at this verse) is to take our needs to the Lord in prayer and give thanks by faith that God has answered. Those who are still burdened have not totally cast their care over on to the Lord. **"Casting all your care upon him; for he careth for you"** (1 Pet. 5:7, underline mine).

LIVING COMMENTARY NOTE:

The Greek word *merimnao*, which was translated **"careful"** in this verse, literally means "to be anxious about" (*Strong's Concordance*). The *New International Version* translated it as **"anxious."** The word *anxious* means "uneasy and apprehensive about an uncertain event or matter; worried" (*American Heritage Dictionary*). This is a command for us not to be anxious about anything. How do we do that? This verse goes on to explain that we are supposed to take our needs and problems to the Lord in prayer. Anxious people are people who haven't thrown their problems over on the Lord in prayer.

Notice that all our supplications are supposed to be made with thanksgiving. That's very important. Sometimes people just tell the Lord all their problems and call that prayer. That's complaining. But when we voice our needs to the Lord and wrap them in thanksgiving, that moves us over into the realm of faith. If there isn't thanksgiving in every prayer we pray, then we aren't abounding in faith (Col. 2:7).

PHILIPPIANS 4:6 *(Continued)*

LIVING COMMENTARY NOTE:

Paul said we are to give thanks when we make our requests to God. A request is something asked for but not yet received. We wouldn't request something to happen that has already happened. So, we are supposed to thank the Lord for doing things before He does them. That's what the Bible calls faith.

Notice we are supposed to use **"prayer and supplication."** Many people only think of prayer as supplication; i.e., asking for something. But the Greek word *proseuche*, translated **"prayer"** in this verse, means "prayer (worship)" (*Strong's Concordance*). This is saying we need to be praising the Lord, which moves us into faith, and then make our supplication to the Lord.

DISCIPLESHIP QUESTIONS

1. What does **"careful"** mean in this verse?

2. How are you to fulfill this command not to be anxious about anything?

3. When you voice your needs to the Lord and wrap them in _____, that moves you over into the realm of _____.

4. *Discussion question:* What are you going to do about burdens in your life?

And the peace of God, which passeth all understanding, shall keep your hearts and minds through Christ Jesus.

PHILIPPIANS 4:7

LIFE FOR TODAY STUDY BIBLE NOTES:

- Notice that peace is the result of casting our care upon the Lord through prayer and thanksgiving (Phil. 4:6). However, many people are asking God to give them peace so that their cares will leave. It doesn't work that way. Through faith, we cast our cares on the Lord, and then God's peace comes.

Christians who are lacking God's peace have not taken their cares to the Lord and left them there. All Christians have peace; it is a fruit of the Spirit that is always present in our born-again spirits (Gal. 5:22). Care will blind us to God's peace. When we eliminate the care, the peace flows.

- Paul was speaking of God's peace, not human peace. Human peace is only experienced in the absence of problems. Therefore, those who only know human peace don't experience it very often, and to a lesser degree. God's peace is independent of circumstances and infinitely greater in supply than any problem we could ever have. God has given us His supernatural peace to enjoy. What a blessing!

- We all have things happen that we don't understand. Those who are relying on themselves can't have any peace in a situation like that. They feel things are out of control, and fear takes over. We believers have God's supernatural peace (see the previous *Life for Today* note at this verse) because we don't have to understand; we trust that God is in control. This is a wonderful difference between true Christians and unbelievers. Faith in God allows us to experience peace that goes beyond our understanding. Praise God!

LIVING COMMENTARY NOTE:

There is a supernatural peace that isn't related to what happens in our lives, and this supernatural peace keeps our hearts and minds at ease. The Greek word that was translated **"shall keep"** is *phroureo*, and it means "to be a watcher in advance, i.e. to mount guard as a sentinel (post spies at gates)" (*Strong's Concordance*).

If we will condition ourselves to always walk in peace, God's peace will protect us. Anytime we begin to lose our peace, we should step back and identify the problem, take evasive action, and always remain in peace. God's peace acts as an umpire in our lives (Col. 3:15).

This peace doesn't just happen, but in context, it is a result of praying about everything and casting our cares over on the Lord (1 Pet. 5:7).

PHILIPPIANS 4:7 *(Continued)*

LIFE FOR TODAY STUDY BIBLE NOTES:

• The peace of God is what keeps our hearts and minds sound. Those who lack peace will be tormented in those areas. Peace is like a fortress against the devil. Before Satan can get to our hearts, he has to get us to step out of God's peace. Therefore, we must let God's peace protect our hearts and minds. **"Let the peace of God rule in your hearts"** (Col. 3:15).

DISCIPLESHIP QUESTIONS

1. What should you do when you start to lose your peace?

2. *Discussion question:* Have you experienced the peace that comes when you cast your care upon the Lord through prayer and thanksgiving? Share an example.

3. Explain the difference between human peace and God's peace.

4. *Discussion question:* This verse says that God's peace will **"keep your hearts and minds through Christ Jesus."** What are your thoughts on this?

Finally, brethren, whatsoever things are true, whatsoever things are honest, whatsoever things are just, whatsoever things are pure, whatsoever things are lovely, whatsoever things are of good report; if there be any virtue, and if there be any praise, think on these things.

PHILIPPIANS 4:8

LIFE FOR TODAY STUDY BIBLE NOTES:

- In closing, Paul admonished the Philippian believers to reflect and meditate upon eight positive principles of thinking that would lead to victorious Christian living (Rom. 8:6). In the Greek, this sentence is constructed in the present imperative, which is a command to do something in the future that involves a continuous and repeated action.

The eight principles of thought to reflect and ponder upon are the following:

1) things that are **"true"**—or honorable, truthful, and upright
2) things that are **"honest"**—or honorable, truthful, genuine, and not characterized by deception or fraud
3) things that are **"just"**—or in accordance with what is right, or right conduct; any circumstance, fact, or deed that is right
4) things that are **"pure"**—or free from defilement or impurity
5) things that are **"lovely"**—or pleasing, agreeable, and inspiring love or affection
6) a **"good report"**—or a saying or report that is positive and constructive, rather than negative and destructive
7) **"virtue"**—or moral excellence, righteousness, and goodness
8) **"praise"**—or what is praiseworthy; expressing one's esteem of others and their virtues

- Notice Paul's use of the word **"whatsoever."** Some Christians think this verse can only be fulfilled by thinking on "church" things or "religious" things, but Paul said **"whatsoever"** falls

LIVING COMMENTARY NOTE:

This relates to what Paul said earlier in this letter about ungodly people minding earthly things (Phil. 3:19). In contrast, we are supposed to keep our focus only on (1) things that are true, (2) things that are honest, (3) things that are just, (4) things that are pure, (5) things that are lovely, (6) things that are of good report, (7) things with virtue, and (8) praise. The *Amplified Bible* ends this verse by saying **"[fix your minds on them]."**

If we would just follow the guidelines of this verse, we would be strong in faith, of little unbelief, not subject to depression, and basically just much more blessed in every respect. Satan gains access to us through the way we think. If all we would think was on these things, then all we could get would be the positive results that these things produce (Rom. 8:6). Peter revealed that it was through seeing and hearing the ungodly people's words and actions, day by day, that Lot vexed his righteous soul (2 Pet. 2:8).

PHILIPPIANS 4:8 *(Continued)*

LIFE FOR TODAY STUDY BIBLE NOTES:

into these eight categories should be the focus of our attention. Therefore, it is not only thinking about spiritual truths that is important; we also need to be able to discern natural truths from lies and think on those things too.

Our lives should not be compartmentalized into *spiritual* and *secular*. Truth is truth whether we are at church or at home. We should think and deal justly whether with our Christian brothers and sisters or with the public on our jobs. We should keep our minds stayed on the good things God has given us in the natural—such as family, health, and work—just as we should think about righteousness, justification, forgiveness, and so forth.

Focusing on the good in every area of our lives is what Paul was advocating. Failure to recognize God's blessings in everyday living will cause us care and anxiety. Recognizing God's hand in even the smallest things will cause peace and will keep our hearts and minds following hard after the Lord.

LIVING COMMENTARY NOTE:

The second thing we are told to think on in this verse is things that are honest. The *New International Version* and *The Message* translated this as **"noble."** The *American Heritage Dictionary* defines *noble* as "having or showing qualities of high moral character." This would exclude most television shows and movies of today. The *American Standard Version* translated this Greek word as **"honorable,"** while the *Amplified Bible* translated it as **"reverence...honorable and seemly."**

The Greek word from which **"just"** was translated means "equitable (in character or act); by implication, innocent, holy" (*Strong's Concordance*).

The Greek word from which **"pure"** was translated means "clean, i.e. (figuratively) innocent, modest, perfect" (*Strong's Concordance*).

DISCIPLESHIP QUESTIONS

1. This verse is constructed in the present imperative. What does that mean?

2. *Discussion question:* Select a few of the qualities listed in this verse. How do they relate (or how should they relate) to your thought life?

3. Your life should not be compartmentalized into what? Why?

Those things, which ye have both learned, and received, and heard, and seen in me, do: and the God of peace shall be with you.

PHILIPPIANS 4:9

LIFE FOR TODAY STUDY BIBLE NOTES:

- Paul listed these four things in reverse order. First of all, the Philippians saw Paul's life. They saw God living through Paul and Silas when the pair came to Philippi and were miraculously delivered from prison through an earthquake (Acts 16:22-31). Next, they heard Paul's message. He used the miraculous events to preach the Gospel and give the glory to Jesus. Third, they received what Paul said and were born again. Then, and only then, they learned Paul's secret of relationship with God by faith in God's grace.

This is a normal progression of events in a person's receiving Christ. If we fail to walk in the supernatural power of God so that unbelievers can see that power in our lives, then few of them will ever stop to hear what we have to say. If they do hear but don't receive, the process stops there. If they receive, then they will learn of Christ personally in an experiential way.

- It is not the hearers of God's Word but the doers of God's Word who are blessed. Paul admonished the Philippians to **do** what they had seen him do. That was no small task. Read what the Lord did through Paul in Philippi (Acts 16).

- Not only were the Philippian believers to think upon whatsoever was true, honest, just, pure, lovely, and of good report (Phil. 4:8), but they were also to "put into practice" the things they had learned. *The Living Bible* renders this verse as **"Keep putting into practice all you learned from me and saw me doing, and the God of peace will be with you."**

LIVING COMMENTARY NOTE:

Once again, Paul was using himself as a role model. This wasn't arrogance. This was wisdom. If what we are teaching isn't working for us, then we shouldn't be teaching it. If what we teach is working for us, then we should be encouraging others to emulate us.

Paul had just told the believers to think on the eight things he listed in Philippians 4:8. Here, he instructed them to follow him because he was doing exactly what he had instructed them to do. He lived what he preached. So should we.

PHILIPPIANS 4:9 *(Continued)*

LIFE FOR TODAY
STUDY BIBLE NOTES:

In this verse, the Greek word *prasso* was translated **"do,"** and *prasso* means "to 'practise'" (*Strong's Concordance*). It is a present imperative (see the first *Life for Today* note at Phil. 4:8), meaning this is "a command to keep on doing an action as one's general habit or lifestyle" (*The Discovery Bible*, Moody Press).

DISCIPLESHIP QUESTIONS

1. If what you are teach is working for you, then what should you do?

2. *Discussion question:* Why or why not do you think using yourself as an example is an effective tool to reach others?

3. Who are the ones who are blessed?

4. *The Living Bible* renders this verse as **"Keep _____ _____ _____ all you learned from me and saw me doing, and the God of peace will be _____ _____."**

But I rejoiced in the Lord greatly, that now at the last your care of me hath flourished again; wherein ye were also careful, but ye lacked opportunity.

PHILIPPIANS 4:10

LIFE FOR TODAY STUDY BIBLE NOTES:

• Paul's conduct with the Corinthian church, where he refused to receive personal offerings (1 Cor. 9:11-18), has been misinterpreted. Some have said that he would not receive offerings from anyone he ministered to; however, that is not true. This verse makes it very clear that he received offerings from the Philippians, and in Philippians 4:16, Paul stated that the Philippians had given to him on at least two other occasions.

Paul's practice of not receiving personal offerings from the Corinthians was the exception and not the rule.

• What Paul meant by saying that the Philippians had been careful was that they had desired to send him another offering. However, because he had been in transit from Caesarea to Rome for a year and communications were much different then than they are now, the Philippians had been unable to locate him. Therefore, they had not had an opportunity to give as they desired.

LIVING COMMENTARY NOTE:

Paul was thanking the Philippians for the way they ministered to him physically. They had desired to do that for a long time, but in those days, they couldn't communicate the way we do today. Paul was in transit to Rome for months, and then once he arrived in Rome, it took time for the Philippians to hear about it. Therefore, their desire was to help Paul, but they just didn't have the opportunity.

Once again, this was one of the things that made the Philippians special to Paul. They weren't like some of the people he had ministered to who only took. These people were givers. This really blessed Paul.

Paul wasn't greatly rejoicing because of the physical gift; he had learned to be content without "things" (Phil. 4:11). He was rejoicing because this revealed their great love for him, and he knew that would produce fruit that would abound to their account (Phil. 4:17).

PHILIPPIANS 4:10 (Continued)

DISCIPLESHIP QUESTIONS

1. Why was Paul rejoicing?

2. *Discussion question:* Why or why not do you feel that giving as the Philippians did is an attitude you need to adopt?

Not that I speak in respect of want: for I have learned, in whatsoever state I am, therewith to be content.

PHILIPPIANS 4:11

LIFE FOR TODAY STUDY BIBLE NOTES:

- Paul did not want the Philippians to draw a wrong conclusion from what he had just said. Although he appreciated the gifts from the saints at Philippi, his needs being supplied was not the source of his joy. Paul knew the secret of contentment: It was finding all of his life in Christ (Heb. 13:5).

- Paul had to **learn** to be content. Contentment doesn't come naturally or as a result of circumstances.

Solomon said in Ecclesiastes 2:24, **"There is nothing better for a man, than that he should eat and drink, and that he should make his soul enjoy good in his labour. This also I saw, that it was from the hand of God"** (underline mine). Solomon went on to say in the next verse, **"For who can eat, or who else can hasten hereunto, more than I?"**

What Solomon was saying was that no one on the earth could indulge his or her desires the way he had. He was the richest man who has ever or will ever live (2 Chr. 1:12), yet he had come to the conclusion that people have to make themselves enjoy life. Things and circumstances didn't satisfy Solomon, and they won't do it for us either. It is a choice on our part.

Paul had **learned** to be content. Every one of us has that capacity, just like we have the intellect to read and write, but reading and writing don't come naturally. We have to learn, and some learn better than others. Likewise, we have to learn to be content, and some learn that lesson better than others.

The secret to Paul's contentment was that he had died to himself and was living totally for

LIVING COMMENTARY NOTE:

It wasn't the physical things that the Philippians had sent to Paul that blessed him. It was the love behind their gifts that touched Paul's heart. Therefore, his thanks weren't just because of the physical things they had provided. Paul was appreciative of their thoughtfulness.

Notice that Paul learned to be content. It didn't just come naturally or as a byproduct of circumstances. Contentment is a choice, a decision. We can teach ourselves to be content.

Paul was in prison in Rome and facing possible execution, but he was content. One of the ways we learn contentment is to be thankful for what we have and quit thinking about what we don't have. Most people in prison would be focused on all the things they can't do. I'm sure Paul was thinking about what he could do. He preached the Gospel to the Jewish leaders in Rome (Acts 28:17-29), which he wouldn't have been able to do without being arrested and transported to Rome. Everyone in the caesar's palace heard the Gospel (Phil. 1:12-18). He had gained the favor of his captors

PHILIPPIANS 4:11 *(Continued)*

LIFE FOR TODAY STUDY BIBLE NOTES:

God (Phil. 1:21 and Gal. 2:20). Paul was dead to himself. It isn't hard to please dead people; they don't have any needs. All depression and discontentment center around selfishness. If we eliminate selfishness, we can be content.

• Paul made special mention that his contentment worked in whatever state he found himself. This means that godly contentment isn't dependent upon circumstances. That is totally opposite of the way most people think today.

No one really desires depression, but very few feel any responsibility or authority to maintain positive emotions in the face of negative circumstances. They think emotions follow circumstances. That's not true. Emotions follow the way we think, and we can choose to think on things that are lovely, true, of good report, and so forth (Phil. 4:8), regardless of our circumstances. As our thinking goes, so go our emotions (Prov. 23:7, Is. 26:3, and Rom. 8:6).

• Paul's priorities were correct. Even though God desires to prosper His people (3 John 2 and 2 Cor. 8:9), Paul's focus was not on possessions but upon Christ (2 Cor. 3:18). Likewise, we should believe that it is the Lord's will to prosper us financially and receive that, but not complain when we find ourselves in difficult situations.

LIVING COMMENTARY NOTE:

so that they gave him his own hired house and the freedom for all his friends to come to him (Acts 28:30). There was complete freedom to preach the Gospel (Acts 28:31), which was more than he experienced in freedom among the Jews. Since the promotion of Jesus was all that mattered to Paul, then things were going better than ever before.

DISCIPLESHIP QUESTIONS

1. You can _____ yourself to be _____.

2. What is one of the ways you learn contentment?

3. *Discussion question:* What are your thoughts on the idea that "As our thinking goes, so go our emotions" and its accompanying verses: Proverbs 23:7, Isaiah 26:3, and Romans 8:6?

I know both how to be abased, and I know how to abound: every where and in all things I am instructed both to be full and to be hungry, both to abound and to suffer need.

PHILIPPIANS 4:12

LIVING COMMENTARY NOTE:

Paul was so dead to his flesh that his physical condition was not a driving force in his life. A few people have majored on being abased to the point that they glory in it. But people who are truly dead to their flesh will be comfortable abounding also. There are ditches on both sides of the road, and there are extremes on both sides of any issue. We always have to strike the balance and stay out of both ditches.

DISCIPLESHIP QUESTIONS

1. *Discussion question:* What do you think of Andrew's commentary on this verse, and how would you explain it to others?

I can do all things through Christ which strengtheneth me.

PHILIPPIANS 4:13

LIFE FOR TODAY STUDY BIBLE NOTES:

- It is not a correct use of this verse to express that we can do anything. This is not a "self-motivational" verse. Paul was saying that he could do anything **through Christ**. That is radically different than the way many people use this verse.

All of our ability in the Christian life is found in Christ. It is not our ability that makes us strong but our availability through Christ that enables us. Paul said, **"For when I am weak, then am I strong"** (2 Cor. 12:10). He was saying that when he recognized his inability and therefore relied on the Lord, the Lord's strength flowed through him.

We can do all things **through Christ**.

LIVING COMMENTARY NOTE:

In context, Paul was speaking about handling the lack and hardships that came along with his ministry. Through Christ, he could overcome all the adversity that came his way. But the same power that sustains us through hardships also enables us to do all things that the Lord leads us to do.

Notice that we can do all things *through Christ*. We are not self-sufficient. And the Lord doesn't just do things for us. It's Christ working through us. We are partners with the Lord.

DISCIPLESHIP QUESTIONS

1. **"I can do all things _____ _____ which strengtheneth me."**

2. Is it correct to use this verse to express that you can do anything?

3. *Discussion question:* How have you ever, like Paul, recognized your inability and therefore relied on the Lord, and His strength flowed through you?

Notwithstanding ye have well done, that ye did communicate with my affliction.

PHILIPPIANS 4:14

LIFE FOR TODAY STUDY BIBLE NOTES:

• Paul had just said that whatever his circumstances were, he was content. He hastened to add that the Philippians had done the right thing in giving toward his needs. The Apostle John said, **"But whoso hath this world's good, and seeth his brother have need, and shutteth up his bowels of compassion from him, how dwelleth the love of God in him?"** (1 John 3:17).

It is godly to give to those in need and especially to ministers who have been a blessing to you (Gal. 6:6). Paul certainly would have given to someone in his situation. It wasn't necessary for Paul to have everything going according to God's perfect plan for him to be content.

• Notice that Paul called his lack of having physical necessities an **"affliction."** Poverty because of the Gospel is an affliction (Ps. 22:24, Is. 63:9, Mark 4:17, 2 Cor. 8:2, and James 1:27).

LIVING COMMENTARY NOTE:

Although Paul had stated that he was content in whatever situation he was in, he didn't want the Philippians to think he didn't appreciate their gifts. They had done the right thing. It's admirable that we bear whatever adversity comes our way, but it's also admirable that we receive the help that's offered to us.

DISCIPLESHIP QUESTIONS

1. It's admirable that you bear whatever adversity comes your way, but what is also admirable?

2. *Discussion question:* How does a give-and-take relationship among believers (giving to those in need, accepting aid in times of need) help strengthen the body of Christ?

3. What does **"affliction"** refer to in this verse?

Now ye Philippians know also, that in the beginning of the gospel, when I departed from Macedonia, no church communicated with me as concerning giving and receiving, but ye only.

PHILIPPIANS 4:15

LIFE FOR TODAY STUDY BIBLE NOTES:

- The *Today's English Version* translated this verse as **"You Philippians know very well that when I left Macedonia in the early days of preaching the Good News, you were the only church to help me; you were the only ones who shared my profits and losses."**

- The word **"communicated"** in this verse was translated from the Greek word *koinoneo*, and this Greek word means "to share with others" (*Strong's Concordance*). It is akin to the word *koinonia* that was translated **"fellowship"** in Philippians 1:5, and *koinonia* means "partnership" (*Strong's Concordance*) (see my note at Phil. 1:5). Paul was speaking of money.

Paul was saying that the Philippians were the only group who gave to him after he left that area. They sent offerings to him twice when he was in Thessalonica. Their thoughtfulness of him and the Gospel he was preaching endeared these Philippians to him and occasioned the writing of this letter (see the *Introduction to Philippians* at the beginning of this book).

LIVING COMMENTARY NOTE:

The Philippians were the biggest givers Paul had. They didn't just support him while he was in Philippi; they sent money to him at least twice when he was in Thessalonica. No other church that he started had done that. Counting this instance, the Philippians sent special offerings to Paul three times that we know of.

Paul was expressing his gratitude to the Philippians, but in doing so, he revealed one of the saddest things in his life, in my opinion. Out of all the places he had been, only one group of people—the Philippians—ever supported him after he left their area. This was a man who suffered as no one else did (2 Cor. 11:23-30), just so others could hear the Good News and be saved. He laid his life down for them, and the majority took what he offered but didn't honor the one who brought these truths to them. May this not be so with me.

DISCIPLESHIP QUESTIONS

1. *Discussion question:* Why or why not do you think it's wrong to have a ministerial relationship with others based on financial support?

2. *Discussion question:* Only the Philippians supported Paul financially once he left their area. What are your thoughts on those other places and people who didn't support Paul once he left?

For even in Thessalonica ye sent once and again unto my necessity.

PHILIPPIANS 4:16

LIFE FOR TODAY STUDY BIBLE NOTES:

- The Philippians sent offerings to Paul twice while he was in Thessalonica. Thessalonica was approximately ninety miles from Philippi.

LIVING COMMENTARY NOTE:

The Philippians supported Paul's ministry at least twice when Paul was in Thessalonica.

DISCIPLESHIP QUESTIONS

1. *Discussion question:* Why do you think the Philippians continued to send Paul offerings?

Not because I desire a gift: but I desire fruit that may abound to your account.

PHILIPPIANS 4:17

LIFE FOR TODAY STUDY BIBLE NOTES:

• It is evident from Paul's statements that he was pleased the Philippians had sent him money. Here, lest he be misunderstood, he gave the real reason that he was so blessed. It was not because he was full (Phil. 4:18); he was content before he received their gifts (Phil. 4:11). It was because he knew how the Philippians' giving would produce **"fruit that may abound to your account."**

This implies that a spiritual account is being kept of our deeds. This would correspond with being judged out of the books that the Lord is keeping (see the last *Life for Today* note at Phil. 4:3). Godly giving—which is giving with the proper motive (1 Cor. 13:3)—makes deposits into that account. It is important to see our giving not as money leaving our lives but as money being deposited into our spiritual accounts. Those deposits go into our future, where they grow and multiply.

This is not to say that there is a one-to-one ratio between the money we have given and what we can expect to receive. The Lord gives a hundredfold interest on gifts that are given in faith (Mark 10:30).

LIVING COMMENTARY NOTE:

Paul wasn't excited about the Philippians' partnership with him in the Gospel because of the benefit it was to him personally; he knew this would produce spiritual fruit that would abound to their account. It was good for them.

Many ministers have not encouraged or received offerings, because they thought receiving offerings was selfish, and they didn't want to promote themselves. But when offerings are received the correct way, they benefit the people who are giving them. Not receiving offerings is wronging the people (2 Cor. 12:13).

DISCIPLESHIP QUESTIONS

1. Was Paul excited about the Philippians' partnership with him in the Gospel because of the benefit it was to him personally?

2. Why is not receiving offerings wronging the people?

3. It is important to see your giving not as money _____ your life but as money being _____ into your _____ account.

But I have all, and abound: I am full, having received of Epaphroditus the things which were sent from you, an odour of a sweet smell, a sacrifice acceptable, wellpleasing to God.

PHILIPPIANS 4:18

LIFE FOR TODAY STUDY BIBLE NOTES:

• Paul was praising God and thanking the Philippians for everything he had received from them. He said he had everything and was full. By his own admission, he was abounding, but we have to remember that he was still in prison and facing possible execution at the hands of the Romans. Most of us wouldn't consider that to be abounding and having everything. This shows that it didn't take much for Paul to be content. Paul's contentment was found in the Lord and not in things (see my note at Phil. 4:11).

• The Philippians' gifts were not only a blessing to Paul but had also blessed God. The Lord loves a cheerful giver (2 Cor. 9:7).

LIVING COMMENTARY NOTE:

The Philippians really blessed the Apostle Paul. What an encouragement this must have been to Paul. He had been in prison for over two years. He had been through rejection and shipwreck. Yet, here were converts through his ministry who pursued him relentlessly until they were able to give to his needs. Thank God for people like this.

See my note on Epaphroditus at Philippians 2:25.

DISCIPLESHIP QUESTIONS

1. Whom did the Philippians' gifts bless?

But my God shall supply all your need according to his riches in glory by Christ Jesus.

PHILIPPIANS 4:19

LIFE FOR TODAY STUDY BIBLE NOTES:

• This verse is often taken out of context to say that the Lord will meet our every need. That is not exactly what Paul was saying. He was speaking to the Philippians who had given to him on more than one occasion (Phil. 4:16). They had, in a sense, made a deposit into a spiritual account (see the *Life for Today* note at Phil. 4:17), and God would use their generosity to multiply their giving toward the meeting of their own needs.

It is God's will to supply all our needs, but it doesn't work without us believing. How is it that we express our faith in the area of finances? It is through giving. It takes faith to give away a portion of what we have and trust that we will have enough. If there were no God and if His promises of multiplying our gifts back to us were not true, it would be stupid to give. If what we have isn't enough, then giving part of that away will leave us with even less.

But there is a God who is true to His promises, and when we give, we express that faith. People who are not giving, because they don't have enough, are people who don't believe. They can say what they want, but that is the bottom line.

The Philippians had proved their faith through their gifts, and Paul was confident that the Lord would meet their every need. Those who are not walking in faith through giving cannot claim this scripture.

• Some people have used the word **"need"** to say that only the bare necessities are covered in this promise. The primary definition of the word *need*, according to the *American Heritage Dictionary*, is "a lack of something required or desirable."

LIVING COMMENTARY NOTE:

This is a great promise, but it is often taken out of context. Paul was saying this to his partners. This doesn't apply to everyone. It is true that the Lord desires to supply the needs of all His children. But not all of us cooperate with Him in this matter of giving and receiving; therefore, it will not happen that all our needs get supplied. When we faithfully give as these Philippians did, though, God's ability is released and His supply manifests.

PHILIPPIANS 4:19 *(Continued)*

LIFE FOR TODAY STUDY BIBLE NOTES:

The word **"supply"** in this verse came from the Greek word *pleroo*, and this Greek word means "to make replete, i.e. (literally) to cram (a net)…satisfy" (*Strong's Concordance*). It is the same word that was used in Philippians 4:18 and translated, **"I am full."** The Lord is speaking of abundance.

The Lord doesn't want us to just barely get along. We can see what the Lord's standard of abundance is when Jesus turned the water into wine (John 2:6), and when He fed the 5,000 (John 6:12) and the 4,000 (Mark 8:8). See also 2 Corinthians 9:8.

• Our needs will be supplied **"according to his riches in glory,"** not according to the current economic status. Sometimes people fear how their needs will be supplied, because of recession, layoffs, or small-town economies. But God uses His resources in glory to meet our needs. We can be assured that there is no shortage there. God's economy is not affected by man's problems.

DISCIPLESHIP QUESTIONS

1. When is God's ability released and His supply manifested?

2. *Discussion question:* What is your perception of this verse, knowing that it was directed to partners (i.e., faithful givers)?

3. *Discussion question:* What are your views on giving, especially in light of what Andrew said in his commentary? Use scriptures to support your response.

4. The word **"supply"** in this verse came from the Greek word *pleroo*, and this Greek word means "to make replete, i.e. (literally) to cram (a net)…satisfy" (*Strong's Concordance*). What does this tell you?

Now unto God and our Father be glory for ever and ever. Amen.

PHILIPPIANS 4:20

LIVING COMMENTARY NOTE:

What a privilege to have God as our Father!

DISCIPLESHIP QUESTIONS

1. *Discussion question:* What does it mean to you to have God as your Father?

Salute every saint in Christ Jesus. The brethren which are with me greet you.

PHILIPPIANS 4:21

LIFE FOR TODAY
STUDY BIBLE NOTES:

• Here, Paul and the brethren with him greeted all of the saints in Christ Jesus. The word **"saint"** is not referring to one's holiness; rather, it is a description of those who belong to Christ.

LIVING COMMENTARY NOTE:

We are to be in relationship with all believers.

DISCIPLESHIP QUESTIONS

1. You are to be in _____ with _____ believers.

2. What is **"saint"** describing in this verse?

All the saints salute you, chiefly they that are of Caesar's household.

PHILIPPIANS 4:22

LIFE FOR TODAY STUDY BIBLE NOTES:

• They that were of **"Caesar's household"** were probably the Christians who were servants in the palace of the emperor. Paul said in the first chapter of this letter (Phil. 1:12-13) that his bonds were known to all who were in the palace. There is no doubt that Paul took this opportunity to preach the Gospel, and this verse makes it clear that some accepted Christ as their Savior.

LIVING COMMENTARY NOTE:

Paul's time in prison in Rome had produced converts in the caesar's own palace. Paul wasn't crying and complaining about his situation. He was rejoicing in his all-expense-paid trip to Rome and the spiritual fruit it had produced. What an attitude.

DISCIPLESHIP QUESTIONS

1. Paul wasn't crying and complaining about his situation—what was he doing instead?

2. *Discussion question:* Why or why not do you think that if you were in prison, you would be sharing the Gospel with those around you?

The grace of our Lord Jesus Christ be with you all. Amen. <<To [the Philippians written from Rome, by Epaphroditus.]>>

PHILIPPIANS 4:23

LIVING COMMENTARY NOTE:

Paul wrote a similar closing in his letter to the Galatians (Gal. 6:18). There he said, **"Brethren, the grace of our Lord Jesus Christ be with your spirit. Amen."**

There are different subscripts attached to this epistle. Most say this was written from Rome and sent by Epaphroditus.

DISCIPLESHIP QUESTIONS

1. *Discussion question:* What are some comparisons and contrasts in the closing statements in Paul's letter to the Philippians and his letter to the Galatians?

2. *Discussion question:* What do you think Paul meant by this closing?

PHILIPPIANS 4
Answer Key

PHILIPPIANS 4:1

1. To see others experience the abundant life that only God can give

2. Make you stand and keep you from falling (Jude 24)

3. *Discussion question*

PHILIPPIANS 4:2

1. Differences / inevitable

2. *Discussion question*

3. To find common ground in the Lord and fellowship in those areas

4. No

PHILIPPIANS 4:3

1. *Discussion question*

2. You cannot enter God's presence without your name being written in the Lamb's Book of Life, and anyone whose name is not written in the Book of Life will spend eternity in the lake of fire

3. Yes

PHILIPPIANS 4:4

1. Happy / rejoice

2. Joy comes from the inside and is a fruit of the Spirit—it is not a response to circumstances

3. Before the Lord our God (Lev. 23:40; Deut. 12:12, and 18), in God's salvation (1 Sam. 2:1), because we are those who seek the Lord (1 Chr. 16:10), in goodness (2 Chr. 6:41), in God's mercy (Ps. 31:7), when we sing to God (Ps. 71:23), because our names are written in heaven (Luke 10:20), in the light (John 5:35), in hope of the glory of God (Rom. 5:2), in the day of Christ (Phil. 2:16), in Christ Jesus Himself (Phil. 3:3), in sufferings (Col. 1:24)

4. *Discussion question*

PHILIPPIANS 4:5

1. *Discussion question*

2. Because **"the Lord is at hand"**

PHILIPPIANS 4:6

1. "To be anxious about" (*Strong's Concordance*), to be full of cares or anxiety

2. You are supposed to take your needs and problems to the Lord in prayer

3. Thanksgiving / faith

4. *Discussion question*

PHILIPPIANS 4:7

1. Step back and identify the problem, take evasive action, and always remain in peace

2. *Discussion question*

3. Human peace is only experienced in the absence of problems—God's peace is independent of circumstances and infinitely greater in supply than any problem you could ever have

4. *Discussion question*

PHILIPPIANS 4:8

1. A command to do something in the future that involves a continuous and repeated action

2. *Discussion question*

3. Spiritual and secular, because truth is truth whether you are at church or at home

PHILIPPIANS 4:9

1. Encourage others to emulate you

2. *Discussion question*

3. Not the hearers of God's Word but the doers of God's Word

4. **"Putting into practice" / "with you"**

PHILIPPIANS 4:10

1. Because the Philippians' giving revealed their great love for him, and he knew that would produce fruit that would abound to their account (Phil. 4:17)

2. *Discussion question*

PHILIPPIANS 4:11

1. Teach / content

2. To be thankful for what you have and quit thinking about what you don't have

3. *Discussion question*

PHILIPPIANS 4:12

1. *Discussion question*

PHILIPPIANS 4:13

1. **"Through Christ"**

2. No

3. *Discussion question*

PHILIPPIANS 4:14

1. That you receive the help that's offered to you

2. *Discussion question*

3. Lack of having physical necessities, poverty because of the Gospel

PHILIPPIANS 4:15

1. *Discussion question*

2. *Discussion question*

PHILIPPIANS 4:16

1. *Discussion question*

PHILIPPIANS 4:17

1. No
2. Because when received the correct way, they benefit the people who are giving them
3. Leaving / deposited / spiritual

PHILIPPIANS 4:18

1. Both Paul and God

PHILIPPIANS 4:19

1. When you faithfully give
2. *Discussion question*
3. *Discussion question*
4. The Lord is speaking of abundance—He doesn't want you to just barely get along

PHILIPPIANS 4:20

1. *Discussion question*

PHILIPPIANS 4:21

1. Relationship / all
2. Those who belong to Christ, not one's holiness

PHILIPPIANS 4:22

1. Rejoicing in his all-expense-paid trip to Rome and the spiritual fruit it produced
2. *Discussion question*

PHILIPPIANS 4:23

1. *Discussion question*
2. *Discussion question*

ABOUT THE AUTHOR

For over four decades, Andrew Wommack has traveled America and the world teaching the truth of the Gospel. His profound revelation of the Word of God is taught with clarity and simplicity, emphasizing God's unconditional love and the balance between grace and faith. He reaches millions of people through the daily *Gospel Truth* radio and television programs, broadcast both domestically and internationally. He founded Charis Bible College in 1994 and has since established Charis Bible College extension schools in other major cities of America and around the world. Andrew has produced a library of teaching materials, available in print, audio, and visual formats. And, as it has been from the beginning, his ministry continues to distribute free audio materials to those who cannot afford them.

RECEIVE JESUS AS YOUR SAVIOR

Choosing to receive Jesus Christ as your Lord and Savior is the most important decision you'll ever make!

God's Word promises **"that if thou shalt confess with thy mouth the Lord Jesus, and shalt believe in thine heart that God hath raised him from the dead, thou shalt be saved. For with the heart man believeth unto righteousness; and with the mouth confession is made unto salvation"** (Rom. 10:9-10). **"For whosoever shall call upon the name of the Lord shall be saved"** (Rom. 10:13).

By His grace, God has already done everything to provide salvation. Your part is simply to believe and receive.

Pray out loud, *"Jesus, I confess that You are my Lord and Savior. I believe in my heart that God raised You from the dead. By faith in Your Word, I receive salvation now. Thank You for saving me!"*

The very moment you commit your life to Jesus Christ, the truth of His Word instantly comes to pass in your spirit. Now that you're born again, there's a brand-new you!

It doesn't really matter whether you felt anything or not when you prayed to receive the Lord. If you believed in your heart that you received, then God's Word promises that you did. **"Therefore I say unto you, What things soever ye desire, when ye pray, believe that ye receive them, and ye shall have them"** (Mark 11:24). God always honors His Word. Believe it!

Please contact me and let me know that you've prayed to receive Jesus as your Savior . I would like to rejoice with you and help you understand more fully what has taken place in your life. *Welcome to your new life!*

RECEIVE THE HOLY SPIRIT

As His child, your loving heavenly Father wants to give you the supernatural power you need to live this new life.

"For every one that asketh receiveth; and he that seeketh findeth; and to him that knocketh it shall be opened...how much more shall your heavenly Father give the Holy Spirit to them that ask him?" (Luke 11:10 and 13).

All you have to do is ask, believe, and receive!

Pray, *"Father, I recognize my need for Your power to live this new life. Please fill me with Your Holy Spirit. By faith, I receive it right now! Thank You for baptizing me! Holy Spirit, You are welcome in my life!"*

Congratulations—now you're filled with God's supernatural power!

Some syllables from a language you don't recognize will rise up from your heart to your mouth (1 Cor. 14:14). As you speak them out loud by faith, you're releasing God's power from within and building yourself up in the spirit (1 Cor. 14:4). You can do this whenever and wherever you like!

It doesn't really matter whether you felt anything or not when you prayed to receive His Spirit. If you believed in your heart that you received, then God's Word promises that you did. **"Therefore I say unto you, What things soever ye desire, when ye pray, believe that ye receive them, and ye shall have them"** (Mark 11:24). God always honors His Word. Believe it!

Please contact me and let me know that you've prayed to be filled with the Holy Spirit. I would like to rejoice with you and help you understand more fully what has taken place in your life. *Welcome to your new life!*

RECOMMENDED MATERIALS

DISCIPLING THROUGH ROMANS
Recently a prisoner shared with me how he and a group of men would gather around in the penitentiary and read Andrew Wommack's *Life for Today* commentary notes. This generated a lot of discussion, and many people were helped through these men's Bible study. So, I decided to put together a combination of *Life for Today* footnotes from the book of Romans along with questions and an answer key. We call this tool *Discipling through Romans*. The beauty of this particular study is that it takes a person verse-by-verse through an entire book of the Bible. In this way, we avoid many of the pitfalls that would emphasize only one particular truth at the expense of another. Expositional teaching is by far a safer approach to examining the Scriptures. I believe that you can adapt this method of study and teaching to your own particular group. You may read my notes and then create a discussion, you could read the notes and then ask the prepared questions, or you could go directly to the Scriptures (read the scripture) and then ask a question. There's a freedom to adapt this study and personalize it in your own particular way.

Item Code: 415 Spiral-Bound

DISCIPLING THROUGH GALATIANS
Throughout the centuries, the church has rediscovered the truths contained within the book of Galatians. These truths have reformed the church, brought revival, and brought the unadulterated truth of the Gospel of God's grace again to the forefront. There is no other book that has changed so many lives as the book of Galatians. It was the first book that was written to an early church that was struggling with the question, "How is man made right with God?"

Discipling through Galatians' verse-by-verse commentary was prepared by Don Krow, a former full-time instructor with Charis Bible College in Colorado Springs, CO. It is a study tool you will want in your library as well as a valuable instrument in bringing the insight of God's grace to others.

Item Code: 416 Spiral-Bound

OTHER RECOMMENDED TEACHINGS

SPIRIT, SOUL & BODY

Understanding the relationship of your spirit, soul, and body is foundational to your Christian life. You will never truly know how much God loves you or believe what His Word says about you until you do. Learn how they're related and how that knowledge will release the life of your spirit into your body and soul. It may even explain why many things are not working the way you had hoped.

Item Code: 1027-C CD album
Item Code: 1027-D DVD album
Item Code: 318 Paperback
Item Code: 418 Companion study guide
Item Code: 701 Spanish book

A SURE FOUNDATION

God's Word is the only true foundation for your life. Listen as Andrew explains the supernatural process that occurs when you plant the Word in your heart. He uses the example of how Jesus dealt with John the Baptist's unbelief to reveal the power of the Word.

Item Code: 1034-C CD album
Item Code: 1034-D DVD album

ETERNAL LIFE

Is eternal life just about living forever, or could there be more? What does God's Word say? Andrew's answer to this question may change the way you view salvation and your approach to your relationship with God.

Item Code: K60-C Single CD

DISCIPLESHIP EVANGELISM

Did God call us to make converts or disciples? It's an important question. The misunderstanding of that has led to some appalling statistics. Many evangelists now realize that only about 15 percent of those who accept Jesus continue in the faith. It's time we changed our thinking and started practicing what Jesus taught. Learn more in this enlightening series.

Item Code: 1069-C CD album
Item Code: 1069-D DVD album

OTHER RECOMMENDED TEACHINGS

THE TRUE NATURE OF GOD
Are you confused about the nature of God? Is He the God of judgment found in the Old Testament or the God of mercy and grace found in the New Testament? Andrew's revelation on this subject will set you free and give you a confidence in your relationship with God like never before. This is truly nearly-too-good-to-be-true news.

Item Code: 1002-C CD album
Item Code: 308 Paperback
Item Code: 743 Spanish book

YOU'VE ALREADY GOT IT!
Are you trying to get the Lord to heal, bless, deliver, or prosper you? If so, stop it! God has already done all He will ever do for you. How can that be? Listen as Andrew teaches on the balance between grace and faith, and you'll understand that you've already got what you need. Never again will you beg God for anything.

Item Code: 1033-C CD album
Item Code: 1033-D DVD album
Item Code: 320 Paperback
Item Code: 420 Companion study guide
Item Code: 732 Spanish book

www.ingramcontent.com/pod-product-compliance
Lightning Source LLC
Chambersburg PA
CBHW080735300426
44114CB00019B/2599